THE TEN-MINUTE GUIDE to
EDUCATIONAL LEADERSHIP

THE TEN-MINUTE GUIDE to EDUCATIONAL LEADERSHIP

A Handbook of Insights

Dr. ROBERT H. PALESTINI

Dean, Graduate and Continuing Studies
Assistant Professor, Educational Leadership
Saint Joseph's University
Philadelphia, Pennsylvania

Rowman & Littlefield Education
Lanham • New York • Toronto • Oxford

This title was originally published by ScarecrowEducation.
First Rowman & Littlefield Education edition 2006.

Published in the United States of America
by Rowman & Littlefield Education
A Division of Rowman & Littlefield Publishers, Inc.
A wholly owned subsidary of The Rowman & Littlefield Publishing Group, Inc.
4501 Forbes Boulevard, Suite 200, Lanham, Maryland 20706
www.rowmaneducation.com

PO Box 317
Oxford
OX2 9RU, UK

British Library Cataloguing in Publication Information Available

The Technomic edition of this book was cataloged as follows by the Library of Congress:
Main entry under title:
   The Ten-Minute Guide to Educational Leadership: A Handbook of Insights
Bibliography: p.
Includes index p. 93
Library of Congress Catalog Card No. 98-60078
ISBN- 13: 978-1-56676-650-0
ISBN- 10: 1-56676-650-8

Contents

.

How often have you visited or heard about educational institutions where there were "tough" administrators, whose institutions seemed to win while the people in them lost? Some of their supervisors thought that they were good administrators, while many of their co-workers and subordinates thought otherwise.

Many of these administrators would depict themselves as autocratic managers who "kept on top of the situation and had everything under control." We have heard pride in their voices as they describe their credo that "Nice guys finish last."

On the other hand, many of us have observed and met many "nice" administrators, whose people seemed to win while their institutions lost. Some of the people who reported to them thought they were effective administrators, but those to whom the administrators reported had their doubts. These administrators would claim that they were "democratic," "participative," even "humanistic." We have heard pride in their voices as they declare themselves "people persons."

It is as though most administrators in the world are primarily interested either in results or people, but not necessarily both. Effective administrators, however, manage themselves and the people they work with so that both their institutions and the people benefit from their presence.

In their extremely enlightening book, *The One Minute Manager*,

Kenneth Blanchard and Spencer Johnson express in allegorical terms the three "secrets" to being an effective manager. The three secrets are as follows:

(1) One-minute goal setting

(2) One-minute praising

(3) One-minute reprimanding

Blanchard and Johnson suggest that taking one minute each day to consider each of these three secrets will result in effective management. Accepting these points as a good beginning, I would suggest that we supplement them with seven more "secrets" of my own. Moreover, I would suggest adding one minute every day to ponder each of the following guidelines to successful administration:

(4) One-minute assessment of structure and culture

(5) One-minute assessment of trust and respect

(6) One-minute assessment of tolerance for change

(7) One-minute assessment of leadership style

(8) One-minute assessment of the communication process

(9) One-minute assessment of the decision-making process

(10) One-minute assessment of the conflict resolution process

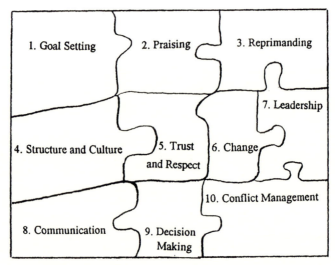

Figure I.1. *The Jigsaw Puzzle of Effective Administration.*

Figure I.1 lists the ten assessments that, when applied in an integrated fashion, complete the jigsaw puzzle of effective school administration.

Picture yourself standing in the middle of a dense forest. Suppose you were asked to describe the characteristics of the forest: what types of trees are growing there? where are the trees thriving? where are they not? Faced with this proposition, most people "would not be able to see the forest for the trees."

Newly appointed, and some not so newly appointed, school administrators often have these same feelings of confusion when faced with the prospect of having to assume a leadership role in complex organizations like schools. Where does one start? An effective way to start would be to examine systematically the components that comprise an organization. Such a system of organizational diagnosis and prescription will lead to a comprehensive and integrated analysis of the organization's strengths and weaknesses and point the way toward improvement. This book suggests such a sequential and systematic approach. Utilizing it effectively can produce dramatic results.

Each chapter of this book is dedicated to one of the ten components of effective school leadership. Most of each chapter focuses on the implementation of these principles, but there is some emphasis on the supporting theory that speaks to why these principles are effective. We know that administrators are busy people; therefore, at the end of each chapter is a diagnostic checklist of questions that should be helpful in quickly assessing the status of these principles in your institution and whether they need to be addressed. It is hoped that addressing these questions in a systematic and concrete way will allow us to see both the forest and the trees.

One-Minute Goal Setting

Blanchard and Johnson posit that the effective manager must spend time developing goals and placing them in the context of a vision. There is much to be said as to the wisdom of this assertion, especially in school settings. There is a plethora of "effective school" research that corroborates their recommendation. Educational researchers, such as John Goodlad and Ernest Boyer, have found that when schools develop clear and agreed-upon goals that are duly promulgated, such schools are usually effective. Thus, effective educational administrators need to develop an educational vision that is mutually acceptable and is understood by all components of the school community.

In some circles exactly what constitutes an educational vision seems to be shrouded in mystery. Actually, the process of developing an educational vision is not all that complex. The first step is to identify a list of broad goals. This step in the process should be done in conjunction with representatives of all components of the school community. Otherwise, there will be no sense of "ownership" on the part of the school community, and its absence will preclude successful implementation of the vision and its goals. "All Children Achieving" is an example of such a broad goal.

The next step in the process is to merge and prioritize the goals and summarize them in the form of a short and concise statement. The following is an example of a vision statement:

1

Our vision for the Exeter School System is that all of our graduating students, regardless of ability, will say, "I have received an excellent education that has prepared me to be an informed citizen and leader in my community." In addition, our students will be committed to a process of lifelong learning and the making of a better world by living the ideals of fairness and justice and service to others.

The key concepts in the above vision statement are "all students can learn," "excellence," "leadership," "lifelong learning," "values," and community "service." It is these concepts or goals that the ten-minute educational leader needs to stress in all forms of communication and in all of his or her interpersonal relations with the various members of the school community.

The final step in the process is the "institutionalizing" of the vision. This step ensures that the vision endures even when the leadership in the institution changes. Operationalizing and placing the important concepts of the vision into the official policies and procedures of the school system is one important way of helping to institutionalize the educational vision and incorporate it into the school culture. Figure 1.1 depicts a typical institutional mission and the objectives, parameters, and strategies that flow from it.

Another way of institutionalizing a vision is by encouraging the development of "heroes" who embody the institution's vision and "tribal storytellers," who promulgate it.[1] We have often heard individuals in various organizations describe a colleague as "an institution around here." Heroes such as these do more to establish the organizational culture of an institution than any manual or policies and procedures handbook ever could. Senior faculty members who are recognized and respected for their knowledge as well as their humane treatment of students are invaluable assets to an educational institution. They are symbols of what the institution stands for. It is the presence of these heroes that sustains the reputation of the institution and allows the workforce to feel good about itself and about where it works. The deeds and accomplishments of these heroes need to be promulgated and become part of the folklore of the institution.

Beliefs

Statements of the schools' and community's fundamental convictions, values, and character.

We believe that:

- The family provides the foundation for the development of the individual.
- The family, community, and school share the responsibility for education, and the student is ultimately responsible for learning.
- Expectation influences achievement.
- Education is vital to a strong, healthy community.
- A safe, positive learning environment is crucial to education.
- Quality education empowers an individual to achieve potential.
- Learning builds self-esteem and self-esteem promotes learning.
- Learning is a life-long process.
- The ability to accept and direct change is vital to continued growth.
- Each individual has dignity and worth.
- Ethical behavior is necessary for a just society.
- All students can learn.
- Students learn at different rates and in different ways.
- The commitment of every person within the organization is essential to its success.

Mission

The mission of the Upper Merion Area School District, in partnership with families and community, is to provide each student with a foundation for life-long learning, to ensure all students are responsible contributors in a rapidly changing society, and to support community needs by providing dynamic leadership, excellent teaching, and diverse, innovative programs.

Objectives

To graduate 100% of our students

To give each graduate the knowledge, skills, and attitudes necessary for life-long learning

To challenge all students to acquire the knowledge and skills necessary to achieve their potential and to pursue their aspirations

To have each student volunteer to provide community service

Figure 1.1. *Upper Merion Area School District Strategic Plan. (Reprinted with permission from James J. Jones and Donald L. Walters.* Human Resource Management in Education. © *1994 by Technomic Publishing Co., Inc., Lancaster, PA.)*

Parameters
1. We will practice participative management at all levels of the organization.
2. No new program or service will be accepted unless
   - it is consistent with the Strategic Plan
   - anticipated benefits clearly justify costs
   - provisions are made for staff development and program evaluation
3. No program or service will be retained unless benefits justify costs and it continues to make a positive contribution to the mission.
4. Nothing will take precedence over the K-12 instructional program.
5. We will not tolerate behavior that demeans the dignity or self-worth of any student, staff, or community member.

Strategies
1. We will foster a climate of trust and cooperation through open communication and participation.
2. We will promote a nonthreatening, caring, disciplined learning environment where mutual respect exists.
3. Using our curriculum as a base, we will identify the outcomes essential for life-long learning and develop means to assess whether students achieve them.
4. We will energize and integrate all aspects of our diverse community to address the social and emotional needs of our students, which are interfering with learning.
5. We will work in partnership with students, parents, and community to establish a volunteer service program to teach all students, at all levels, the value of community service.
6. We will develop and implement plans to set challenging and appropriate expectations for every student (student expectations, parent expectations, and staff expectations).
7. We will examine alternative methods of financing and managing revenue and resources.
8. We will identify and implement a variety of effective instructional techniques and support services, so that 100% of our students graduate, have the knowledge and skills required for life-long learning, and realize their potential.

Figure 1.1 continued. *Upper Merion Area School District Strategic Plan. (Reprinted with permission from James J. Jones and Donald L. Walters.* Human Resource Management in Education. © *1994 by Technomic Publishing Co., Inc., Lancaster, P.A.)*

4

The deeds of these heroes are usually perpetuated by the "tribal storytellers" in an organization. These are the individuals who know the history of the organization and relate it through stories of its former and present heroes. An effective leader encourages the tribal storytellers, knowing that they are providing an invaluable service to the institution. They work at the process of institutional renewal. They allow the institution to improve continuously. They preserve and revitalize the values of the institution. They mitigate the tendency of institutions, especially educational institutions, to become bureaucratic. Every institution has heroes and storytellers. It is the educational leader's job to see to it that things like manuals and handbooks don't replace them.

DIAGNOSTIC CHECKLIST

Here are a few questions that you can address in assessing your institution's understanding of and commitment to its goals:

- Does a mission statement exist?
- Does a vision statement exist?
- Does a strategic plan exist?
- Are the goals and objectives clear and measurable?
- Are they known and understood by the school community?
- Is the planning process ongoing?

Chapter 2

One-Minute Praising and One-Minute Reprimanding

Blanchard and Johnson suggest that managers utilize praising and reprimanding as motivational devices in an organization. This suggestion flows from the first "secret" of effective management, goal setting. Goal-setting theory suggests that setting difficult but attainable goals that are mutually agreed upon can be a powerful motivator.[2] Setting goals like higher reading scores on standardized tests or lower teacher absenteeism help focus behavior and motivate individuals to achieve the desired end. However, in order for goal setting to be an effective motivator, the individual involved needs feedback on whether movement toward attaining the goal is adequately progressing.

This is where one-minute praisings and reprimands come in. It is important that the administrator keep his or her staff abreast of the adequacy of their performance. When they are very specific and clear, both praise and reprimands can be effective sources of motivation. As Blanchard and Johnson point out, however, one should "never attack a person's worth or value as a person."[3] Reprimand the behavior only, not the person. Thus, the feedback and the individual's reaction to it is about the specific behavior and not their feelings about themselves as human beings.

It is always a good idea to follow a reprimand with a praising. Make certain that the staff member knows that his or her behavior is not okay, but that he or she is okay. According to Blanchard and Johnson, the one-minute manager should not be Nice 'n' Tough, but rather, Tough 'n' Nice.[4]

Reinforcement theory applies behaviorist learning theories to motivation and has implications for the effectiveness of praisings and reprimands.[5] This theory emphasizes the importance of feedback and rewards in motivating desired behavior through diverse reinforcement techniques, including positive reinforcement, like praise, and punishment, like reprimands. The schedule of reinforcement also affects the effectiveness of the motivational process. Table 2.1 shows examples of the various types of reinforcement schedules.

Positive reinforcement involves actively encouraging a desired behavior by repeated praisings of desired behaviors or outcomes with rewards or feedback. This feedback "shapes" behavior by encouraging the reinforced or rewarded behavior to recur. If the behavior is not precisely what is desired by the administrator, repeated reinforcements resulting in successive approximations to the desired behavior can move the actual behavior closer to the desired behavior. For example, if a principal desires more interactive classroom instruction from a teacher, the principal might compliment the teacher when a cooperative learning activity is part of the lesson plan, and when

Table 2.1. Reinforcement Schedules.

	Fixed	Variable
Interval	Reinforcement or reward given after the first proper response following a specified period of time	Reinforcement or reward given after a certain amount of time with that amount changing before the next reinforcement
	Weekly or monthly paycheck	Supervisor who visits shop floor on different unannounced days each week
		Unexpected merit bonuses
Ratio	Reinforcement or reward given after a specified number of proper responses	Reinforcement or reward given after a number of responses with that number changing before the next reinforcement
	Pay for piecework	Praise

Source: Adapted from Judith Gordon. *Organizational Behavior*. Boston: Allyn & Bacon (1993).

other interactive techniques are used, additional praise may be given. Praise and other incentives are used until the best performance occurs.

Punishment, on the other hand, actively eliminates undesirable behaviors by applying an undesirable reinforcer (reprimand) to an undesirable behavior. Although it can be effective in eliminating undesirable behavior, punishment can produce anger and bitterness and be counterproductive in the long run. This is why the administrator must be careful to reprimand infrequently, and when doing so, to reprimand the undesirable behavior and not the individual. It is also the reason that, when possible, a reprimand of the behavior should be followed by a praising of the individual. "Your lesson plan for today was somewhat poorly conceived, but I know that you have the ability to do better" is an example of reprimanding the behavior and praising the individual.

DIAGNOSTIC CHECKLIST

Here are some questions that might be addressed in assessing your institution's motivational processes:

- Do the rewards satisfy the variety of individual needs?
- Are rewards both internal and external?
- Are they applied equitably and consistently?
- Do individuals value the rewards they receive?
- Do they perceive that their efforts correlate with performance?
- Do individuals set goals as a source of motivation?
- Are the rewards and incentives effective in motivating desired behaviors?

Chapter 3

One-Minute Assessment of Structure and Culture

The educational leader should take one minute each day to assess the current state of the institution's structure and its culture. Every salesperson is advised to get to "know the territory." The astute administrator will take a page from *The Music Man*'s Professor Hill and get to know the territory in his or her educational institution. Knowing the territory in education translates into being keenly aware of the organizational structure and culture of the institution.

Educational entities are essentially organized according to one of three basic structures: the classical structure, the social systems structure, or the open systems structure. Despite being organized around one of these structures, most schools and school systems reflect certain aspects of each of these models.[6] These structures are illustrated in Figure 3.1.

Classical theorists believe that an application of a bureaucratic structure and process will promote rational, efficient, and disciplined behavior, making possible the achievement of well-defined goals. Efficiency, then, is achieved by arranging positions and jurisdiction and by placing power at the top of a clear chain of command. The conceptual model of the classical theory has had a significant impact on education. Virtually every school and school system in the United States is organized according to the tenets of the classical theory. Table 3.1 lists the various classical principles that have been adopted by educational institutions.

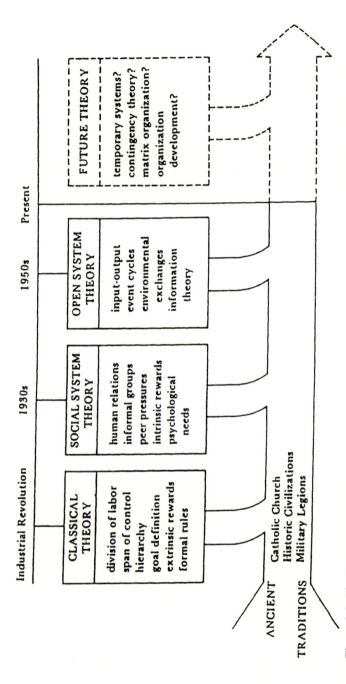

Figure 3.1. *The Evolution of Organization Theory. (Adapted with permission from Billy Hodge and Herbert Johnson. Management and Organizational Behavior: A Multidimensional Approach. New York: John Wiley & Sons, 1970, p. 19.)*

12

Table 3.1. Scientific Management Principles Applied to Schools.

Scientific Management Principles	Adaptation to Education
Formation of a hierarchy with graded levels of authority	Levels of control: superintendent to assistant superintendent to principals to vice-principals to teachers to students.
Scientific measurement of tasks and levels of performance	Students thoroughly tested in subject areas, aptitude, and achievement and classified by levels of learning.
Shape unity of ends (of managers and workers)	Conventional wisdom in schools dictates that teachers and administrators have the same objective: doing what is best for kids.
Define a scientific order of work	Third-grade knowledge is differentiated and preparatory to fourth-grade knowledge which is differentiated and preparatory to fifth-grade knowledge, and so on.
Establish a division of labor	English teachers, history teachers, coaches, teacher aides, janitors, administrators, and so on.
Determine appropriate span of control	Thirty elementary students per teacher, 20 high school students per teacher, four vice-principals per principal.
Adhere to the chain of command	Teachers must first talk with the principal before going to see the superintendent.
Define rules of behavior	Teachers' handbook: "All teachers will be in their rooms by 8:00 A.M. and are obligated to remain on the school premises until 3:30 P.M. Teachers will stand outside their rooms and monitor the passing of students between periods. A copy of all messages being sent by teachers to parents must be on file at the principal's office.
Establish discipline among the employees	Students will abide by the rules of the school and the norms of good conduct. Teachers will adhere to the policies of the district and the norms of the teaching profession.
Recruitment based on ability and technical knowledge	Teaching and/or administrative credentials required for certification to enter the field.
Define the one best way of performing a task	Schools continually search for the best way of teaching reading, mathematics, history, and the like.

Source: Adapted from Mark Hanson. *Educational Administration and Organizational Behavior.* Boston: Allyn & Bacon (1991).

13

Within the classical theory framework, the individual is regarded as an object, a part of the bureaucratic machine. This is the antithesis of the second organizational theory, the social systems theory. Historically, researchers found that the impact of social-psychological variables within the worker group was significant. The study of behavior in social system settings intensified, and a greater sophistication developed about how and why group members behave as they do under given conditions. In time a natural social systems orientation to the analysis of behavior evolved in the literature as an alternative to the rational or classical systems approach.

The conceptual perspective of the social systems model suggests that an organization consists of a collection of groups (social systems) that collaborate to achieve system goals. Coalitions among subgroups within the organization, e.g., English teachers, history teachers, and foreign language teachers, form to provide power bases upon which positive or negative action can be taken; for example, "Let's all vote to reject writing behavioral objectives." As with the classical organizational theory, schools and school systems have been profoundly influenced by the social systems model.

A newer theory that is having a growing influence on educational institutions, especially higher education, is the open systems model. The classical and social systems theories tend to view organizational life as a closed system, isolated from the surrounding environment. In contrast, open systems theory regards an organization as a set of interrelated parts that interact with the environment. It receives "input" such as human and material resources, values, community expectations, and societal demands, transforms them through a production process (an educational program), and exports the product in the form of "output" (graduates, new knowledge, revised value sets) into the environment (businesses, the military, homes) with "value added." The organization receives a return (community financial support in the form of taxes or tuition) for its efforts so it can survive and prosper. Then the cycle begins once again. Figure 3.2 illustrates the open systems dynamic.

Through the perspective of open systems theory, a new logic on issues of organizational governance has emerged. It emphasizes the relationship of the organization to its surrounding environment and

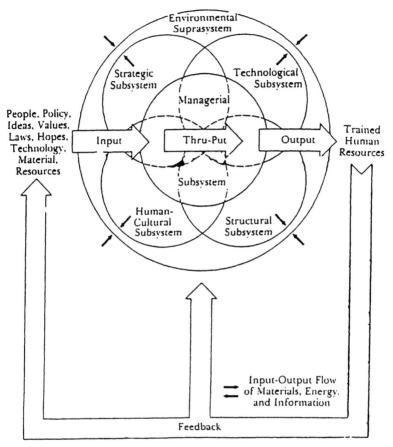

Figure 3.2. *Open System Mode. (Adapted from* Contingency Views of Organization and Management, *from Fremont E. Kast and James E. Rosenzweig, Science Research Associates, Inc., 1973. Reprinted by permission of the authors.)*

thus places a premium on planning and programming for events that cannot be controlled directly. The key to making an open system work effectively and efficiently is its ability to gather, process, and utilize information. In an educational institution, then, the facility with which a need is discovered, a goal is established, and resources are coalesced to meet that need will determine the effectiveness and efficiency of that institution. Unlike businesses, educational institutions, especially colleges and universities, have not yet found a way to meet the demands of the open system model.

Knowing how one's educational entity is structured within the context of these three models is the first step in an educational leader's quest to truly "know the territory." The second step is to be aware of the organizational behavior or culture of the institution. Organizational culture is composed of the shared beliefs, expectations, values, and norms of conduct of its members. In any organization, the informal culture interacts with the formal structure and control system to produce a generally clear understanding of the "way things are done around here." Even more than the forces of bureaucracy, the organization's culture is the glue that binds people together.

Anyone who has visited a number of school develops a sense of their different "personalities" or culture. Walking the hallways and campus of an educational institution, an astute observer can see physical manifestations of an underlying set of values: perhaps a huge trophy case in the entrance lobby, classroom desks bolted to the floor, a clean and attractive campus, football and basketball programs that overshadow math and science programs, faculty and staff constantly patrolling the halls, clandestine meetings of students or faculty, and so forth.

The above are tangible aspects of the school's culture. The intangible aspects often parallel those values. Schools attempting to develop shared values and enculturate them often illustrate them by symbols frequently found around the campus: "Knowledge Is Power," "Wildcat Pride," "Education Is about Alternatives," "Just Say No," and "All Children Achieving." Other symbols of the school's culture are the heroes and storytellers that we mentioned earlier.

Administrators can influence the institution's structure and culture in a positive way. First, however, they must be aware of its importance and its components. If the educational leader has a thorough knowledge of the institution's culture, he or she can set about trying to influence it. One way of doing so is to take time each day to review this and the nine other "secrets" to effective school management that are presented in this book.

DIAGNOSTIC CHECKLIST

Here are some questions that can be addressed in assessing your institution's structure and culture:

- Is there appropriate division of labor and is it flexible?
- Is the division of labor conducive to reaching organizational goals?
- Is the structure of the organization well designed?
- Do work groups operate effectively?
- Are the best aspects of the classical, social systems, and open systems organizational structures present?
- Does the organization's structure respond to the environmental contingencies?
- Does the organization exhibit a culture of mutual trust and respect?
- Do perceptual distortions proliferate?
- Does the workforce exhibit an internal locus of control?
- Is the institution a learning organization?
- Are the various learning styles being addressed in the management process?
- What beliefs and values do the individuals in the organization have?
- How do these beliefs and values influence individual attitudes?
- What functional and dysfunctional behaviors result from the individual's attitudes?

Chapter 4

One-Minute Assessment
of Trust and Respect

These are exciting times in education. Revolutionary steps are being taken to restructure schools and rethink the teaching-learning process. The concepts of empowerment, total quality management, the use of technology, and strategic planning are becoming the norm. However, while these activities have the potential to influence education in significantly positive ways, they must be based upon a strong foundation to achieve their full potential.

Achieving educational effectiveness is an incremental, sequential improvement process. This improvement process begins by building a sense of security within each individual so that he or she can be flexible in adapting to changes within education. Addressing only skills or techniques, such as communication, motivation, negotiation, or empowerment, is ineffective when individuals in an organization do not trust its systems, themselves, or one another. An institution's resources are wasted when invested only in training programs that assist administrators in mastering quick-fix techniques that at best attempt to manipulate and at worst reinforce mistrust.

The challenge is to transform relationships based on insecurity, adversarialism, and politics to those based on mutual trust. Trust is the beginning of effectiveness and forms the foundation of a principle-centered learning environment that places emphasis upon strengths and devises innovative methods to minimize weaknesses.

19

The transformation process requires an internal locus of control that emphasizes individual responsibility and accountability for change and for promoting effectiveness.

For many of us, there exists a dichotomy between how we see ourselves as persons and how we see ourselves as workers. In the words of a Zen Buddhist: "The master in the art of living makes little distinction between his work and his play, his labor and his leisure, his mind and his body, his education and his recreation, his love and his religion. He hardly knows which is which. He simply pursues his vision of excellence in whatever he does, leaving others to decide whether he is working or playing. To him he is always doing both."

Work can be and should be productive, rewarding, enriching, fulfilling, and joyful. Work is one of our greatest privileges, and it is up to leaders to make certain that work is everything that it can and should be.

One way to think of work is to think of how a philosopher would lead an organization, rather than how a business executive would lead an organization. Plato's *Republic* speaks of the "philosopher-king," where the king would rule with the philosopher's ideals and values. Taking such an approach engenders trust.

Paramount among the ideals that leaders need to recognize in leading an organization is the notion of teamwork and the valuing of each individual's contribution to the final product. The synergy produced by an effective team is greater than the sum of its parts.

The foundation of the team is the recognition that each member needs every other member and that no individual can be successful without the cooperation, trust, and respect of others. As a young boy I was a very enthusiastic baseball fan. My favorite player was the Hall of Fame pitcher Robin Roberts of the Philadelphia Phillies. During the early 1950s his fastball dominated the National League. My uncle, who took me to my first ballgame, explained that opposing batters were so intimidated by Roberts's fastball that they were automatic "outs" even before they got to the plate. My uncle claimed that Robin Roberts was unstoppable. Even as a young boy I intuitively knew that no one was unstoppable by himself. So I said to my uncle that I knew how to stop Robin Roberts: "Make me his catcher."

Our institutions will not amount to anything without the people who make them what they are. And the individuals most influential in making institutions what they are, are essentially volunteers. Our very best teachers and administrators can work anywhere they please. So, in a sense, they volunteer to work where they do. As educational leaders, we would do far better if we looked upon and treated our employees as volunteers. To engender trust and respect, then, we should treat our employees as if we had a covenantal relationship rather than a contractual relationship with them.[6]

Alexander Solzhenitsyn, speaking to the 1978 graduating class of Harvard University, said this about legalistic relationships: "A society based on the letter of the law and never reaching any higher, fails to take advantage of the full range of human possibilities. The letter of the law is too cold and formal to have a beneficial influence on society. Whenever the tissue of life is woven of legalistic relationships, this creates an atmosphere of spiritual mediocrity that paralyzes men's noblest impulses. . . . After a certain level of the problem has been reached, legalistic thinking induces paralysis; it prevents one from seeing the scale and the meaning of events."

Covenantal relationships, on the other hand, induce freedom, not paralysis. As the noted psychiatrist William Glasser explains: "Coercion only produces mediocrity; love or a sense of belonging produces excellence." Our goal as leaders is to encourage a covenantal relationship of love, warmth, and personal chemistry among our employee volunteers. Shared ideals, shared ideas, shared goals, shared respect, a sense of integrity, a sense of quality, a sense of advocacy, a sense of caring—these are the basis of an institution's covenant with its employees.

We often hear administrators suggest that a new program does not have a chance of succeeding unless the teachers and the staff take "ownership" of it. Most of us agree to the common sense of such an assertion. But how does a leader promote teacher/staff ownership? Let me suggest four steps as a beginning.

(1) Respect people. As we have indicated earlier, this starts with appreciating the diverse gifts that individuals bring to an institution. The key is to dwell on the strengths of your colleagues rather than on their weaknesses. Try to turn their weaknesses into strengths.

This does not mean that disciplinary action or even dismissal will never become necessary. What it does mean, however, is that we should focus on the formative aspect of the employee evaluation process before we engage in the summative part.

(2) Let belief guide policy and practice. We spoke earlier of developing a culture of civility in your institution. If there is an environment of mutual trust and respect, I believe that the institution will flourish. Leaders need to let their belief or value system guide their behavior. Style is merely a consequence of what we believe and what is in our hearts.

(3) Recognize the need for covenants. Contractual agreements cover such items as salary, fringe benefits, and working conditions. They are an important part of organizational life and there is a legitimate need for them. But in today's educational institutions, where the best people working for these institutions are like volunteers, we need covenantal relationships. As we said, our best workers may choose their employers. They usually choose the institution where they work based on reasons less tangible than salaries and fringe benefits. They do not need or seek contracts; they need and seek covenants.

Covenantal relationships enable educational institutions to be civil, hospitable, and understanding of individuals' differences and unique characteristics. They allow administrators to recognize that treating everyone equally is not necessarily treating them equitably or fairly.

(4) Understand that culture counts more than structure. An educational institution that I have been associated with, recently went through a particularly traumatic time when the credibility of the administration was questioned by the faculty and staff. Various organizational consultants were interviewed as facilitators of a "healing" process. Most of the consultants spoke of making the necessary structural changes to create a culture of trust and respect. We finally engaged a consultant whose attitude was that organizational structure has nothing to do with trust. Interpersonal relations based on mutual respect and an atmosphere of good will are what create a culture of trust. The structure is secondary to the processes used in an institu-

tion. The healing had to begin by analyzing the communication, decision making, conflict resolution, and planning processes, not by analyzing the organizational structure. Ask yourself the question: "Would you rather work in an educational institution with an outstanding reputation or work as part of a group of outstanding individuals?" Many times these two characteristics go together, but if one had to choose, I believe that one would opt to work with outstanding individuals.

If an educational institution is to be successful in creating a culture of trust and respect, everyone in it needs to feel like he or she "owns the place." "This is not the school district's school; it is not the board of directors' school; it is *my* school." Taking ownership is a sign of one's love for an institution. In his book, *Servant Leadership*, Robert Greenleaf says, "Love is an undefinable term, and its manifestations are both subtle and infinite. It has only one absolute condition: unlimited liability!" Although it may run counter to our traditional notion of American capitalism, employees should be encouraged to act as if they "own the place." It is a sign of love.

DANGER SIGNS

Up to now we have dwelled on the characteristics of a healthy educational institution, one that embodies mutual trust and respect. In contrast, the following are some of the signs that the institution is suffering from the lack of these qualities:

- when there is a tendency merely to "go through the motions"
- when a dark tension exists among key individuals
- when a cynical attitude prevails among co-workers
- when finding time to celebrate accomplishments becomes problematic
- when stories and storytellers are nowhere to be found
- when there is the view that one person's gain needs to be at another's expense
- when leaders accumulate power rather than distribute it
- when attainment of short-term goals becomes detrimental to the acquisition of long-term goals

- when individuals abide by the letter of the law, but not the spirit
- when people treat students as impositions
- when the accidents become more important than the substance
- when the loss of grace, style, and civility occur
- when leaders use coercion to motivate employees
- when administrators dwell on individuals' weaknesses rather than their strengths
- when individual turf is protected to the detriment of institutional goals
- when diversity and individual talents are not respected
- when communication is only one-way
- when employees feel exploited and manipulated
- when arrogance spawns top-down decision making
- when leaders prefer to be served rather than to serve

In our discussion so far, we have suggested that educational leaders are made, not born. We posited that if one could master the "secrets" involved in effective leadership, one could become a successful leader. Here, however, we make the argument that learning the skills involved in effective leadership is only part of the story. Leadership is as much an art, a belief, a condition of the heart, as it is a set of skills. A truly successful leader, therefore, is one who leads with both the mind and the heart. It is only then that a sense of mutual trust and respect can be established in an institution. And since it all starts with trust, it is only then that the educational leader can hope to be successful.

Chapter 5

One-Minute Assessment
of Leadership Styles

Leadership is offered as a solution for most of the problems of organizations everywhere. Schools will work, we are told, if principals provide strong instructional leadership. Around the world, administrators and managers say that their organizations would thrive if only senior management provided strategy, vision, and real leadership. Though the call for leadership is universal, there is much less clarity about what the term means.[7] Figure 5.1 gives a rather inclusive definition of leadership.

Historically, researchers in this field have searched for the one best leadership style that would be most effective. Current thought is that there is no one best style. Rather, a combination of styles depending on the situation the leader finds himself or herself in has been found to be more appropriate. To understand the evolution of leadership theory thought, we will take an historical approach and trace the progress of leadership theory beginning with the trait perspective of leadership and moving to the more current contingency theories of leadership.

Trait theory suggests that we can evaluate leadership and propose ways of leading effectively by considering whether an individual possesses certain personality traits, social traits, and physical characteristics. Popular in the 1940s and 1950s, trait theory attempted to predict which individuals successfully became leaders and then

25

LEADERSHIP

is the *Ability* to establish and *Manage*

a *Creative Climate*

where people are *Self-Motivated*

toward the *Achievement*

of long term *Goals*

in an environment of *Mutual Respect*,

compatible with personal *Values*.

Figure 5.1. Leadership Definition.

whether they were effective. Leaders differ from non-leaders in their drive, desire to lead, honesty and integrity, self-confidence, cognitive ability, and knowledge of the business that they are in.

Limitations in the ability of trait theory to predict effective leadership caused researchers during the 1950s to view a person's behavior rather than personal traits as a way of increasing leadership effectiveness. This view also paved the way for later situational theories.

The types of leadership behaviors investigated typically fell into two categories: production-oriented and employee-oriented. Production-oriented leadership, also called concern for production, initiating structure, or task-focused leadership, involves acting primarily to get the task done. An administrator who tells his or her department chair to do everything they need to get the curriculum developed on time for the start of school demonstrates production-oriented leadership. So does an administrator who uses an autocratic style or fails to involve workers in any aspect of decision making. Employee-oriented leadership, also called concern for people or consideration, focuses on supporting the individual workers in their activities and involving the workers in decision making. A principal who demonstrates great concern for his or her teachers' satisfaction with their duties and commitment to their work has an employee-oriented leadership style.

Contingency or situational models differ from the earlier trait and behavioral models in asserting that no single way of leading works in all situations. Rather, appropriate behavior depends on the circumstances at a given time. Effective managers diagnose the situation, identify the leadership style that will be most effective, and then determine whether they can implement the required style. Early situational research suggested that subordinate, supervisor, and task considerations affect the appropriate leadership style in a given situation. The precise aspects of each dimension that influence the most effective leadership style vary.

Research suggests that the effect of leader behaviors on performance is altered by such intervening variables as the effort of subordinates, their ability to perform their jobs, the clarity of their job responsibilities, the organization of the work, the cooperation and cohesiveness of the group, the sufficiency of resources and support provided to the group, and the coordination of work group activities with those of other subunits. Thus, leaders must respond to these and broader cultural differences in choosing an appropriate style. A leader-environment-follower interaction theory of leadership notes that effective leaders first analyze deficiencies in the follower's ability, motivation, role perception, and work environment that inhibit performance and then act to eliminate these deficiencies.[8] The situational nature of leadership style is illustrated in Table 5.1.

Bolman and Deal have developed a unique situational leadership theory, which analyzes leadership behavior through four frames of reference: structural, human resource, political, and symbolic. Each of the frames offers a different perspective on what leadership is and how it operates in organizations. Each can result in either effective or ineffective conceptions of leadership.

Structural leaders develop a new model of the relationship of structure, strategy, and environment for their organizations. They focus on implementation. The right answer helps only if it can be implemented. Structural leaders sometimes fail because they miscalculate the difficulty of putting their design in place. They often underestimate the resistance that it will generate, and they take few steps to build a base of support for their innovations. In short, they are often undone by human resource, political, and symbolic considerations. Structural leaders continually experiment, evaluate, and adapt, but

Table 5.1. *Effective Leadership Styles under Different Conditions.*

Sample Situational Characteristics	Leadership Styles			
	Directive	Supportive	Achievement	Participative
Task				
Structured	No	Yes	Yes	Yes
Unstructured	Yes	No	Yes	No
Clear goals	No	Yes	No	Yes
Ambiguous goals	Yes	No	Yes	No
Subordinates				
Skilled in task	No	Yes	Yes	Yes
Unskilled in task	Yes	No	Yes	No
High achievement needs	No	No	Yes	No
High social needs	No	Yes	No	Yes
Formal Authority				
Extensive	No	Yes	Yes	Yes
Limited	Yes	Yes	Yes	Yes
Work Group				
Strong social network	Yes	No	Yes	Yes
Experienced in collaboration	No	No	No	Yes
Organizational Culture				
Supports participation	No	No	No	Yes
Achievement oriented	No	No	Yes	No

because they fail to consider the entire environment in which they are situated, they sometimes are ineffective.

Human resource leaders believe in people and communicate that belief. They are passionate about "productivity through people." They demonstrate this faith in their words and actions and often build it into a philosophy or credo that is central to their vision of their organizations. Human resource leaders are visible and accessible. Peters and Waterman popularized the notion of "management wandering around," the idea that managers need to get out of their offices and interact with workers and customers. Many educational administrators have adopted this aspect of management.

Effective human resource leaders empower, that is, they increase participation, provide support, share information, and move decision making as far down the organization as possible. Human resource leaders often like to refer to their employees as "partners" or "colleagues." They want to make it clear that employees have a stake in the organization's success and a right to be involved in making decisions. When they are ineffective, however, they are seen as naive or weak.

Political leaders clarify what they want and what they can get. Political leaders are realists above all. They never let what they want cloud their judgment about what is possible. They assess the distribution of power and interests. The political leader needs to think carefully about the players, their interests, and their power; in other words, he or she must map the political terrain. Political leaders ask questions such as whose support do I need? how do I go about getting it? who are my opponents? how much power do they have? what can I do to reduce the opposition? is the battle winnable? However, if ineffective, these leaders are perceived as being untrustworthy and manipulative.

The symbolic frame provides a fourth turn of the kaleidoscope of leadership. In this frame, the organization is seen as a stage, a theater in which every actor plays certain roles and attempts to communicate the right impressions to the right audiences. The main premise of this frame is that whenever reason and analysis fail to contain the dark forces of ambiguity, human beings erect symbols, myths, rituals, and ceremonies to bring order, meaning, and predictability out of chaos and confusion.

The Bolman and Deal leadership concepts are summarized in Table 5.2.

Transforming leaders are visionary leaders, and visionary leadership is invariably symbolic. Examination of symbolic leaders reveals that they follow a consistent set of practices and rules.

Transforming leaders use symbols to capture attention. When Diana Lam became principal of the Mackey Middle School in Boston in 1985, she knew that she faced a substantial challenge. Mackey had all the usual problems of urban public schools: decaying physical plant, lack of student discipline, racial tension, troubles with the teaching staff, low morale, and limited resources. The only good news was that the situation was so bad that almost any change would have been an improvement. In such a situation, symbolic leaders will try to do something visible, even dramatic, to let people know that changes are on the way. During the summer before she assumed her duties, Lam wrote a letter to every teacher to set up an individual meeting. She traveled to meet teachers wherever they wanted, driving two hours in one case. She asked teachers how they felt about the school and what changes they wanted.

Lam also felt that something needed to be done about the school building, because nobody likes to work in a dumpy place. She de-

Table 5.2. Reframing Leadership.

Effective Leadership	Structural	Human Resource	Political	Symbolic
Leader is:	Social architect	Catalyst, servant	Advocate	Prophet or Poet
Leadership process:	Analysis, design	Support, empowerment	Advocacy, coalition building	Inspiration, framing experience

Ineffective Leadership	Structural	Human Resource	Political	Symbolic
Lead is:	Petty tyrant	Wimp, pushover	Con artist, hustler	Fanatic, fool
Leadership process:	Management by detail and fiat	Management by abdication	Management by fraud, manipulation	Management by mirage, smoke, and mirrors

Source: Adapted from L. Bolman and T. Deal. *Reframing Organization.* San Francisco, CA: Jossey-Bass (1992).

cided that the front door and some of the worst classrooms had to be painted. She had few illusions about getting the bureaucracy of the Boston public schools to provide painters, so she persuaded some of her family members to help her do the painting. When school opened, students and staff members immediately saw that things were going to be different, if only symbolically. Perhaps even more importantly, staff members received a subtle challenge to make a contribution themselves.

Each of the frames captures significant possibilities for leadership, but each is incomplete. In the early part of the century, leadership as a concept was rarely applied to management, and the implicit models of leadership were narrowly rational. In the 1960s and 1970s, human resource leadership became fashionable. The literature on organizational leadership stressed openness, sensitivity, and participation. In recent years, symbolic leadership has moved to center stage, and the literature now offers advice on how to become a visionary leader with the power to transform organizational cultures. Organizations do need vision, but it is not their only need and not always their most important one. Leaders need to understand their own frame and its limits. Ideally, they will also learn to combine multiple frames into a more comprehensive and powerful style.

TRANSFORMATIONAL LEADERSHIP

Charismatic or transformational leaders use charisma to inspire their followers. They talk to the followers about how essential their performance is, how confident they are in the followers, how exceptional the followers are, and how they expect the group's performance to exceed expectations. Lee Iacocca, in industry, and the late Marcus Foster and Notre Dame's Reverend Theodore Hesburgh, in education, are examples of this type of leader. Such leaders use dominance, self-confidence, a need for influence, and conviction of moral righteousness to increase their charisma and consequently their leadership effectiveness. The behavioral components of charismatic and non-charismatic leaders are depicted in Table 5.3.

A transformational leader changes an organization by recognizing an opportunity and developing a vision, communicating that vision to

Table 5.3. Behavioral Components of Charismatic and Noncharismatic Leaders.

	Noncharismatic Leader	Charismatic Leader
Relation to status quo	Essentially agrees with status quo and strives to maintain it	Essentially opposed to status quo and strives to change it
Future goal	Goal not too discrepant from status quo	Idealized vision which is highly discrepant from status quo
Likeableness	Shared perspective makes him/her likable	Shared perspective and idealized vision makes him/her a likable and honorable hero worthy of identification and imitation
Trustworthiness	Disinterested advocacy in persuasion attempts	Disinterested advocacy by incurring great personal risk and cost
Expertise	Expert in using available means to achieve goals within the framework of the existing order	Expert in using unconventional means to transcend the existing order
Behavior	Conventional, conforming to existing norms	Unconventional or counternormative
Environmental sensitivity	Low need for environmental sensitivity to maintain status quo	High need for environmental sensitivity for changing the status quo
Articulation	Weak articulation of goals and motivation to lead	Strong articulation of future vision and motivation to lead
Power base	Position power and personal power (based on reward, expertise, and liking for a friend who is a similar other)	Personal power (based on expertise, respect, and admiration for a unique hero)
Leader-follower relationship	Egalitarian, consensus seeking, or directive	Elitist, entrepreneur, and exemplary
	Nudges or orders people to share his/her views	Transforms people to share the radical changes advocated

Source: Adapted from Judith Gordon. Organizational Behavior. Boston: Allyn & Bacon (1993).

organizational members, building trust in the vision, and achieving the vision by motivating organizational members. The leader helps subordinates recognize the need for revitalizing the organization by developing a felt need for change, overcoming resistance to change, and avoiding quick-fix solutions to problems. Encouraging subordinates to act as devil's advocates with regard to the leader, building networks outside the organization, visiting other organizations, and changing management processes to reward progress against competition also help them recognize a need for revitalization. Individuals must disengage from and disidentify with the past, as well as view change as a way of dealing with their disenchantments with the past or the status quo. The transformational leader creates a new vision and mobilizes commitment to it by planning or educating others. He or she builds trust through demonstrating personal expertise, self-confidence, and integrity. The charismatic leader can also change the composition of the team, alter management processes, and help organizational members reframe the way they look at an organizational situation. The charismatic leader must empower others to help achieve the vision. Finally, the transformational leader must institutionalize the change by replacing old technical, political, cultural, and social networks with new ones. For example, the leader can identify key individuals and groups, develop a plan for obtaining their commitment, and institute a monitoring system for following the changes. If an administrator wishes to make an innovative program acceptable to the faculty and the school community, for example, he or she should follow the above plan and identify influential individuals who would agree to champion the new program, develop a plan to gain support from others in the community through personal contact or other means and develop a monitoring system to assess the progress of the effort.[9]

A transformational leader motivates subordinates to achieve beyond their original expectations by increasing their awareness about the importance of designated outcomes and ways of attaining them, by getting workers to go beyond their self-interest to that of the team, the school, the school system and the larger society, by changing or expanding the individual's needs. Subordinates report that they work harder for such leaders. In addition, such leaders are judged higher in leadership potential by their subordinates as compared to the more common transactional leader.

One should be cognizant, however, of the negative side of charismatic leadership, which may exist if the leader overemphasizes devotion to himself or herself, makes personal needs paramount, or uses highly effective communication skills to mislead or manipulate others. Such leaders may be so driven to achieve a vision that they ignore the costly implications of their goals. The superintendent who overexpands his or her jurisdiction in an effort to form an "empire," only to have the massive system turn into a bureaucratic nightmare, is an example of transformational leadership gone sour. Nevertheless, recent research has verified the overall effectiveness of transformational leadership style.

IMPLICATIONS FOR EDUCATION

The implications of leadership theory for educational administrators are clear. The successful administrator needs to have a sound grasp of leadership theory and the skills to implement it. The principles of situational and transformational leadership theory are guides to effective administrative behavior. The leadership behavior applied to an inexperienced faculty member may be significantly different from that applied to a more experienced and tested one. Task behavior may be appropriate in dealing with a new teacher, while relationship behavior may be more appropriate when dealing with a seasoned teacher.[10]

The four frames of leadership discussed by Bolman and Deal may be particularly helpful to school administrators. Consideration of the structural, human relations, political and symbolic implications of our leadership behavior can keep an administrator attuned to the various dimensions affecting appropriate leadership behavior. With the need to deal with collective bargaining entities, school boards, and a variety of other power issues, the political frame considerations may be particularly helpful in understanding the complexity of relationships that exist between administrators and these groups. Asking oneself the questions posed earlier under the political frame can be an effective guide to the appropriate leadership behavior in dealing with these groups.

Recently, a plethora of research studies have been conducted on leadership and leadership styles. The overwhelming evidence indicates that there is no single leadership style that is most appropriate in all situations. Rather, an administrator's leadership style should be adapted to the situation so that at various times task behavior or relationship behavior might be appropriate. At other times and in other situations, various degrees of both task and relationship behavior may be most effective.

The emergence of transformational leadership has seen leadership theory come full circle. Transformational leadership theory combines aspects of the early trait theory perspective with the more current situational or contingency models. The personal charisma of the leader, along with his or her ability to formulate an educational vision and to communicate it to others, determines the transformational leader's effectiveness.

Since the effective leader is expected to adapt his or her leadership style to an ever-changing environment, administration becomes an even more complex and challenging task. However, a thorough knowledge of leadership theory can make some sense of the apparent chaos that the administrator faces on almost a daily basis.

Take a minute or so each day to empower someone on your staff. Take a minute to assess the maturity level or readiness level of a member of your staff. Mental activities such as these will allow administrators to adapt their leadership styles appropriately to the situation and make an accurate assessment of this "secret" to effective school management.

DIAGNOSTIC CHECKLIST

Here are some questions that may be helpful in assessing the effectiveness of the leadership in your institution:

- Do the administrators display the behaviors required for effective leadership?
- Do the leaders encourage the appropriate amount of participation in decision making?
- Does the leadership adapt to the task and the maturity level of the followers?
- Do transformational leaders exist?
- Do they operate in all four frames of organizational leadership?

Chapter 6

One-Minute Assessment of Tolerance to Change

Changing an educational institution or system has been likened to making a U-turn with the *Queen Elizabeth II.* In some cases, resistance to change is so extreme that this comparison can be considered an understatement.

Despite its difficulty, the process of change is absolutely necessary if an organization is to continually improve. Thus, to be an effective leader, especially in the transformational style, an administrator must become a change agent and master the process that can bring it about effectively.

MODELS OF CHANGE

Suppose the Washington School received a mandate to introduce school-based management, the objective of which was to empower a team of faculty and staff to assist the administration in the operation of the school. And suppose the principal, Rita Curran, had successfully run the school in a relatively autocratic manner for the last 10 years. The faculty leader of the school-based management team was Jodi Jones, who felt that giving the staff a voice in decision making was long overdue.

How will the Washington School move to school-based management? What changes will be required? Who will implement them?

What resistance will they face? These are just a few of the questions that need to be posed and answered if the Washington School is to move successfully toward school-based management. In order to bring about this change effectively, a model of planned change needs to be developed.

The model of planned change suggested here includes seven steps that reflect a systematic approach to introducing change. These steps include assessment, entry, diagnosis, planning, action, evaluation, and termination. Although this model was developed more than two decades ago, it remains a robust and useful approach to introducing change and implementing action in organizations.

The first step in the process is assessment. Change begins by obtaining preliminary information about those involved in the change situation. In particular, the person or group responsible for making the changes or for ensuring that they occur must assess the organization's readiness for change, including a consideration of the environment in which it functions and the nature of its work force. In the case of the Washington School, Rita Curran, Jodi Jones, and the others involved in the school-based management must assess the organization before implementing the new form of administration. They might consider, for example, how the various members of the faculty and staff will react when given the news that such a change will be taking place. They might also wish to collect data on the workforce's openness to change and engage in a full needs assessment process.

The change agent next attempts to negotiate a formal or informal agreement with the organization. In the entry phase, the change agent identifies a reasonable point or person of contact in the organization and then must develop an effective working relationship with him or her or with the group or committee responsible for the change. In the situation at Washington, for example, proponents of school-based management must talk to faculty, staff, administrators, and parents about its proposals for the school and ideally secure their approval of and commitment to the change. Organizational members who will serve as the primary implementers of change, such as those on the school-based management committee, must be identified.

The diagnosis step involves problem definition, further goal specification, and an evaluation of the resources available to deal with the problem. It is during this phase that a force field analysis can be helpful. We will discuss this technique later.

During the planning phase, the change agent and client generate alternative strategies for meeting the objectives of the change. They outline the prescription for change, determine the steps in its implementation, and detail the nature, cost, timing, and personnel required for any new system. This step also requires anticipating and planning for all possible consequences of the change effort. Jodi Jones or other faculty members might take major responsibility for planning action, repeatedly testing support for the proposed action with the rest of the school's faculty, staff, and parents.

In the action phase, the change agent, Jodi Jones, Rita Curran, other faculty and administration, parents, or top administrators in the school system implement the best strategies that arise out of the planning phase.

The change agent collects data about the nature and effectiveness of the change as it occurs. The results of the evaluation indicate whether the change process is complete or whether a return to an earlier stage should occur. The criteria for success should be specified in advance of a change effort; these criteria may be culturally linked and varied. If ineffective outcomes result from the introduction of school-based management, the process should return to an earlier stage; for example, assessment (to determine if the client is really committed to the change), diagnosis (to determine the real nature of the problems), or planning (to determine the best strategy for meeting the change objectives).

During the termination phase, plans for continuing the change into the future or for knowing when it will end should be specified. Ensuring the institutionalization of effective changes should also occur as part of this step. Successful changes should become institutionalized; that is, the changed processes should be established as permanent ways of operating; otherwise, when the present change agent leaves, the change may not be perpetuated. Ideally, the change should become part of the organizational culture. Failures may terminate the change process or may signal a need for other changes, such as different staffing activities, a new reward system, or new technology.

Whatever model is chosen, the change process calls for understanding and changing the forces that affect the change. We can use an analytical technique called force field analysis, which views a problem as a product of forces working in different, often opposite, directions. An organization, or any of its subsystems, will maintain the status quo when the sum of opposing forces is zero. When forces in one direction exceed forces in the opposite one, the organization or subsystem will move in the direction of the greater forces. For example, if the forces for change exceed the forces against change, then change likely will occur.

To move an organization toward a different desired state requires either increasing the forces for change in that direction, decreasing the forces against change in that direction, or both. Generally, reducing resistance creates less tension in the system and fewer unanticipated consequences than increasing forces for change. At the Washington School, for example, reducing the resistance to the changes created by the introduction of school-based management increases the likelihood of the changeover. Figure 6.1 shows what happens when a resistance force is eliminated. When the administrators and staff no longer resist change, the present state, as shown by the solid vertical line, moves closer to the desired state, as indicated by the broken vertical line. A complete analysis looks at ways to alter all forces, for and against change.

Let us consider again the situation at the Washington School. School-based management focused on changing school governance to greater participation by more diverse constituencies; it meant removing some control from the school principal and other top administrators. What forces for change, also known as driving forces, existed? Increased demands for parental involvement, an increasingly complex educational situation, and changes in state legislation are among the forces that might have spurred the change.

Changes in the organization's environment, such as new laws or regulations, rapidly increasing competition, or an unpredictable rate of inflation, may require the organization to implement new structures or reward systems. New programs resulting from the availability of improved technology, changes in competition in the field, or unusual requirements of the new generation of students, like inclusion or mainstreaming, may also affect the institution.

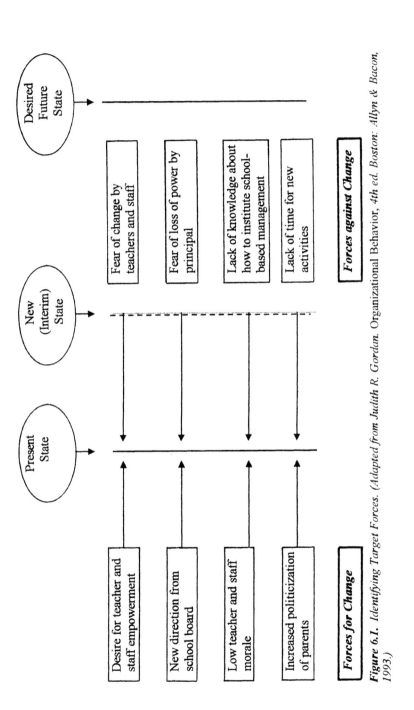

Figure 6.1. *Identifying Target Forces. (Adapted from Judith R. Gordon. Organizational Behavior, 4th ed. Boston: Allyn & Bacon, 1993.)*

41

Finally, reduced productivity and effectiveness, product quality, satisfaction, commitment, or increased turnover or absenteeism may call for changes in intra- or interdepartmental relations. Frequently, one or two specific events external to the organization precipitate the change. For example, the publication of *A Nation at Risk* in the 1980s, caused a flurry of educational changes and reforms that continue until today.

Forces known as resistance forces counteract the forces for change. Administrators might resist changes in their routines and supervisory activities; they may also be unwilling to relinquish their decision-making authority. Superintendents may be unwilling to allocate the resources required to change the culture. Identifying and then reducing resistance forces may be essential to making an individual or group receptive to change. The typical sources of resistance to change are illustrated in Figure 6.2.

Forces against change often reside within the organization and stem from rigid organizational structures and rigid individual thinking. Specific forces against change include employees' distrust of the change agent, fear of change, desires for maintaining power, and complacency; lack of resources to support the change; conflicts between individual and organizational goals; and organizational inertia against changing the status quo. These forces frequently combine into significant resistance to change.

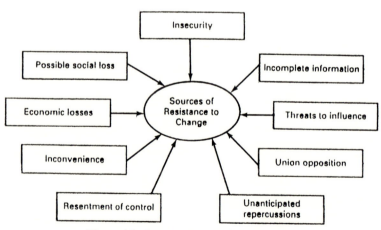

Figure 6.2. Sources of Resistance to Change.

Resistance results from a variety of factors. First, it occurs when a change ignores the needs, attitudes, and beliefs of organizational members. If teachers, for example, have high security needs, they may perceive as threatening the increased attention to distance learning. Second, individuals resist change when they lack specific information about the change; they may not know when, how, or why it is occurring. Third, individuals may not perceive a need for change; they may feel that their organization is currently operating effectively and efficiently. In these cases change often is neither voluntary nor requested by organizational members. Fourth, organizational members frequently have a "we/they" attitude which causes them to view the change agent as their enemy, particularly when change is imposed by representatives outside of the immediate work site. Fifth, members may view change as a threat to the prestige and security of the institution. They may perceive the change in procedures or policies as a commentary that their performance is inadequate. Sixth, employees may perceive the change as a threat to their expertise, status, or security. The introduction of a new computer-aided instructional system, for example, may cause teachers to feel that they lack sufficient knowledge to perform their jobs. The revision of an organization's structure may challenge their relative status in the organization, as our example of site-based management might do. The introduction of a new reward system may threaten their feelings of job security. For effective change to occur, the change agent must confront each of these factors and overcome the resulting resistance to change. It helps a great deal if the change agent has engendered a sense of mutual trust and respect among his or her colleagues before the effort to effect change begins.

BUILDING AN ACTION PLAN

Following the identification of the forces for and against change, the person responsible for implementing the change must identify alternative actions for changing each force and then organize them into an action plan. The analytical approach we are describing here must be supplemented with a consideration of individuals' psychological reactions to change and development of appropriate strategies for dealing with them. The approach can also use action research methodology as a basis of studying and intervening in organizational situations. In action research, the change agent collaborates extensively with the client in gathering and feeding back data. Together they collect and discuss the data and then use the data for planning.[11]

Consider the possible reluctance of the principal to reduce his or her involvement in decision making, a force against change in the school. The following actions could reduce this reluctance: implementing the change slowly, educating the principal about the value of the change, or testing an experimental version of new procedures to increase teacher and staff participation. Another intervention would be to identify a school where site-based management has been successful and have the principal visit that school (best practices approach). An example of an analysis of target forces affecting change at the Washington School is illustrated in Table 6.1.

Overcoming resistance to change is a key action issue for administrators or external change agents. Employees can sabotage change efforts and ultimately decrease their effectiveness. Resistance to change can result in behavior ranging from lowered productivity, increased absenteeism, and decreased motivation. In the extreme, it can lead to work stoppages. The change agent must plan ways to overcome resistance to change like that depicted in Figure 6.3.

The person responsible for change should maintain open and frequent communication with the individuals, groups, or organizations involved. For example, he or she might schedule regular informational meetings for all employees affected by the change. The change agent should also consider the needs of individual employees because responding to needs when possible helps develop in the individuals a vested interest in and ultimately support for the change. Finally, where possible, the change agent should encourage voluntary change. Establishing a climate of innovation and experimentation can reduce the organization's tendency to maintain a status quo.

Development of an action plan concludes with a specification of each action in the order it will be performed. You can continue the analysis for the Washington School or try a similar analysis with an organizational change situation you have faced. Be sure to perform all the steps described above. Figure 6.4 summarizes these steps.

Table 6.1. An Example of an Analysis of Target Forces at the Washington School.

Target Forces	Alternate Actions	Feasibility	Action Priority
Fear of change by the principal, teachers, and staff	Implement change slowly	Moderate; change can occur over a 12-month period	High
	Educate workers about the change	High; easy and relatively low cost	High
	Illustrate the benefits of the new system	High; easy and relatively low cost	High
	Pilot-test the system for small group	Moderate; time-consuming and pilot may be difficult to design	Medium-high
	Involve employees in planning the change	High; time-consuming but important to acceptance	Medium
Lack of knowledge about how to institute new system	Offer training in culture change	High; important to eventual implementation	High
	Provide new policies and procedures	High; important to system implementation	Medium

45

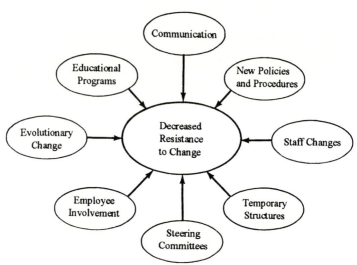

Figure 6.3. *Overcoming Resistance to Change. (Adapted from Gerard C. Ubber and Larry W. Hughes.* The Principal, *3rd ed. Boston: Allyn & Bacon, 1995.)*

1. Identify forces for change.
2. Identify forces against change.
3. Brainstorm actions to reduce forces against change.
4. Brainstorm actions to enhance forces for change.
5. Assess feasibility of each action specified.
6. Prioritize actions.
7. Build an action plan from ranking of actions.
8. Develop timetable and budget for action plan.

Figure 6.4. *Summary of Steps in Change.*

Edwards Deming said that healthy organizations are ones that are continually improving. Continual improvement assumes change. Therefore, if an educational leader is to be effective, he or she must become an agent of change.

Mastering the change process requires a leader to know and understand the steps involved in planning a successful transformation in an organization. If the change can take place in an atmosphere of mutual trust and respect, its chances for success are maximized.

A common model for effecting change is to access the organization to ascertain the need for change, to diagnose the forces that influence change, and to implement the change by maximizing the forces in favor of the change and minimizing the forces opposing the change.

Once the change is made, a thorough evaluation of its effectiveness precedes the final step of institutionalizing the change, which ensures its continuation even after the change agent is no longer present.

The key step in the process is the diagnosing of the forces influencing change. A useful technique in assessing these factors is called force field analysis. This technique allows one to determine the forces in favor of and opposed to change and to plan interventions that would mobilize the forces in favor of change and mitigate the forces opposing change. If one can effectively orchestrate this step of the process, the desired change will most likely occur. In many ways, successfully effecting the process of change necessitates the collective use of all of an administrator's abilities and skills. It can be seen as the culminating activity of an effective administrator and leader.

DIAGNOSTIC CHECKLIST

Here are some questions that can be addressed in assessing an institution's ability to change:

- Are the steps of the rational change model implemented?
- Is a force field analysis used during the change process?
- Are appropriate change agents identified?
- Are intervention strategies appropriate for the situation?
- Do mechanisms exist for institutionalizing the change?

Chapter 7

One-Minute Assessment of the Communication Process

One of the perennial complaints of school personnel is a lack of communication between themselves and another segment of the school community. Oftentimes, the greatest perceived "communications gap" is between the faculty and the administration. If an administrator is to be effective, then he or she must master the skill of effective communication.

Feedback is perhaps the most important aspect of the communications process. Feedback refers to an acknowledgment by the receiver that the message has been received; it provides the sender with information about the receiver's understanding of the message being sent.

Often, one-way communication occurs between administrators and their colleagues. Because of inherent power differences in their positions, administrators may give large quantities of information and directions to their faculty and staff without providing them the opportunity to show their understanding or receipt of the information. These managers often experience conflict between their role as authorities and a desire to be liked by their colleagues. Other administrators have relied on the use of written memoranda as a way of communicating with faculty and staff. In addition to the inherent lack of feedback involved in this method, the use of a single channel of communication also limits the effectiveness of communication. The proliferation of the use of e-mail has alleviated this problem somewhat by providing a relatively facile feedback mechanism.

Why do administrators sometimes not involve their faculty and staff in two-way communication? In some instances, administrators do not trust their colleagues to contribute effectively. In other situations, lack of self-confidence on the part of the administrator makes him or her appear uninterested in others' opinions. Or administrators assume that their faculty and staff have the same goals as they do and thus feel that input from colleagues is not required or would not add anything of significance to the process.

What is your attitude toward feedback? You can assess it by completing the questionnaire shown in Figure 7.1. The higher your score, the more discomfort you feel in getting feedback. Recognizing discomfort about giving or receiving feedback is a key step in eliminating this barrier and improving the quality of managerial communication. Encouraging feedback from others helps show them that you are concerned about them as individuals in ways that go beyond merely ensuring that they produce.

Subordinates also have responsibility for encouraging two-way communication. While managers may attempt to protect their power positions, subordinates attempt to protect the image their supervisor holds of them. Frequently, for example, assistant superintendents may withhold negative information about themselves or their activities. Or they may fail to inform the superintendent about their needs and values. Other subordinates mistrust their superiors and so withhold information from them. Why do these situations arise? Some subordinates may assume that they and their bosses have different goals. Others mistrust their bosses. Still others lack persistence in seeking responses from their supervisors. Impression of management, therefore, plays a key role in whether individuals send feedback. They may assess in what way asking for feedback will be interpreted and how the resulting information will affect each person's public image. In order for effective communication to take place, then, subordinates must show that they, too, are willing to build relationships with their superiors.

What can individuals do to improve their communication in both formal and informal settings? In this section we examine three ways

Indicate the degree of discomfort you would feel in each situation given below, by circling the appropriate number:
1—high discomfort; 2—some discomfort; 3—undecided; 4—very little discomfort; 5—no discomfort.

1.	Telling an employee who is also a friend that he or she must stop coming to work late.	1	2	3	4	5
2.	Talking to an employee about his or her performance on the job.	1	2	3	4	5
3.	Asking an employee if he or she has any comments about your rating of his or her performance.	1	2	3	4	5
4.	Telling an employee who has problems in dealing with other employees that he or she should do something about it.	1	2	3	4	5
5.	Responding to an employee who is upset over your rating of his or her performance.	1	2	3	4	5
6.	An employee's becoming emotional and defensive when you tell him or her about mistakes in the job.	1	2	3	4	5
7.	Giving a rating that indicates improvement is needed to an employee who has failed to meet minimum requirements of the job.	1	2	3	4	5
8.	Letting a subordinate talk during an appraisal interview.	1	2	3	4	5
9.	An employee's challenging you to justify your evaluation in the middle of an appraisal interview.	1	2	3	4	5
10.	Recommending that an employee be discharged.	1	2	3	4	5
11.	Telling an employee that you are uncomfortable in the role of having to judge his or her performance.	1	2	3	4	5
12.	Telling an employee that his or her performance can be improved.	1	2	3	4	5
13.	Telling an employee that you will not tolerate his or her taking extended coffee breaks.	1	2	3	4	5
14.	Telling an employee that you will not tolerate his or her making personal telephone calls on company time.	1	2	3	4	5

Figure 7.1. *Attitude toward Feedback: Feedback Questionnaire.* (Source: *Judith R. Gordon,* Organizational Behavior: A Diagnostic Approach, s/e, © 1996. Reprinted by permission of Prentice Hall, Upper Saddle River, New Jersey.)

of increasing communication effectiveness: creating a supportive communication climate, using an assertive communication style, and using active listening techniques.

In communicating with their faculties and staffs, administrators know they must create a trusting and supportive environment. Creating such a climate has the objective of shifting from evaluation to problem solving and formation in communication. They must avoid making employees feel defensive, that is, threatened by the communication. They can create such an atmosphere in at least six ways:[12]

(1) They use descriptive rather than evaluative speech and do not imply that the receiver needs to change. An administrator may describe teacher traits in terms of strengths and areas in need of further development, rather than describing them as weaknesses.

(2) They take a problem solving orientation, which implies a desire to collaborate in exploring a mutual problem, rather than try to control or change the listener. An administrator can ask the teacher what he or she hopes to achieve in the lesson, or for the academic year, rather than setting out a list of goals for the teacher.

(3) They are spontaneous, honest, and open rather than appearing to use "strategy" that involves ambiguous and multiple motivations. A superintendent might share with the school community the need for restructuring and possible areas of downsizing rather than doing so surreptitiously.

(4) They convey empathy for the feelings of their listener, rather than appearing unconcerned or neutral about the listener's welfare. They give reassurance that they are identifying with the listener's problems, rather than denying the legitimacy of the problems. When reviewing a union grievance with a teacher, the principal may indicate sensitivity to the teacher's position even though the decision may ultimately go against the teacher.

(5) They indicate that they feel equal rather than superior to the listener. Thus they suggest that they will enter a shared relationship, not simply dominate the interaction. A college dean may come out from behind his or her desk and sit next to a colleague to indicate a relationship of equality.

(6) Finally, they communicate that they will experiment with their own behavior and ideas, rather than be dogmatic about them. They do not give the impression that they know all the answers and do not need help from anyone. An administrator can concede that he or she does not know if his or her suggestion will work but ask that the employee in question "try it."

In addition, supportive communication emphasizes a congruence between thoughts and feelings and communication. An individual who feels unappreciated by a supervisor, for example, must communicate that feeling to the supervisor, rather than deny it or communicate it inaccurately. Communication must also validate an individual's importance, uniqueness, and worth. Nondefensive communication recognizes the other person's existence; recognizes the person's uniqueness as an individual, rather than treating him or her as a role or a job; acknowledges the worth of the other person; acknowledges the validity of the other person's perception of the world; expresses willingness to be involved with the other person, at least during the communication.

Interpersonal communication can be improved by encouraging individuals to communicate using as complete knowledge of themselves and others as possible. The Johari window provides an analytical tool that individuals can use to identify information that is available for use in communication. Figure 7.2 illustrates this model of interpersonal knowledge.[10] Note that information about an individual is represented along two dimensions: (1) information known and unknown by the self and (2) information known and unknown by others.

	Known by Self	Unknown by Self
Known by Others	Open self	Blind self
Unknown by Others	Concealed self	Unknown self

Figure 7.2. Johari Window. (Source: Based on a model developed by Drs. Joseph Luft and Harry Ingham and described in The Personnel Relations Survey by Jay Hall and Martha S. Williams, Telometrics International, The Woodlands, Texas.)

Together these dimensions form a four-category representation of the individual. The open self is information known by the self and known by others. The blind self is information unknown by the self and known by others, such as others' perceptions of your behavior or attitudes. The concealed self is information known by you and unknown by others. Secrets we keep from others about ourselves fall into this category. Finally, the unconscious self is information that is unknown to the self and unknown to others. To ensure quality communication, in most cases an individual should communicate from his or her open self to another's open self and limit the amount of information concealed or in the blind spot. Guarded communication may be appropriate, however, if one party has violated trust in the past, if the parties have an adversarial relationship, if power and status differentials characterize the culture, if the relationship is transitory, or if the corporate culture does not support openness.

THE ASSERTIVE COMMUNICATION STYLE

An assertive style, which is honest, direct, and firm, also improves communication. With this style a person expresses personal needs, opinions, and feelings in honest and direct ways and stands up for his or her rights without violating the other person's rights. Assertive behavior is reflected in the content and the nonverbal style of the message. The assertive delegator, for example, "is clear and direct when explaining work to subordinates, doesn't hover, [and] . . . criticizes fairly, objectively, and constructively."[13]

Consider the situation of a superintendent whose assistant has missed two important deadlines in the past month. How would she respond assertively? She might say to her assistant, "I know you missed the last two deadlines. Is there an explanation I should know? It is important that you meet the next deadlines." Her assertive response can include the expression of anger, frustration, or disappointment, but is couched in terms that would allow for feedback to obtain the employee's explanation for the behavior. This distinguishes it from an aggressive style, which is inappropriate behavior.

We can further contrast the assertive approach to nonassertive and aggressive styles. Nonassertive communication describes behavior in which the sender does not stand up for personal rights and indicates that his or her feelings are unimportant; the person may be hesitant, apologetic, or fearful. In the situation of a missed deadline, nonassertive behavior might involve saying nothing to your assistant, hoping the situation would not recur. Individuals act nonassertively because they may mistake assertion for aggression, mistake nonassertion for politeness or being helpful, refuse to accept their personal rights, experience anxiety about negative consequences of assertiveness, or lack assertiveness skills.[14]

Aggressive communication stands up for an individual's rights without respecting the rights of the other person. Aggressive behavior attempts to dominate and control others by sounding accusing or superior. In the situation of the missed deadlines, an aggressive response might be, "You always miss deadlines. You're taking advantage of me and the situation. If you miss another deadline, disciplinary action will be taken." While such a response may result in the desired behavior in the short run, its long-term consequences likely will be dysfunctional, resulting in distrust between the individuals involved. Ultimately, such behavior will negatively affect productivity and will especially affect the submission of creative and innovative solutions offered to management by the employee.

USING ACTIVE LISTENING TECHNIQUES

Active listening, which requires understanding both the content and the intent of a message, can be facilitated by paraphrasing, perception checking, and behavior description. Table 7.1 illustrates the various types of listening.

The receiver can paraphrase the message conveyed by the sender. For example, if the sender states, "I don't like the work I am doing," the receiver might paraphrase it as, "Are you saying that you are dissatisfied with the profession of education? Or are you dissatisfied with the grade that you teach? Or do you wish to be reassigned to another school?" Note that these ways of paraphrasing the original message suggest very different understandings of the original statement. The sender, upon receiving this feedback from the receiver, can then clarify his or her meaning.

Table 7.1. Types of Listening.

Type	Function	Example
Directing	Leads the speaker by guiding the limits and direction of conversation.	If I were you, I'd just ignore it.
Judgmental	Introduces personal value judgments into the conversation; injects personal values or opinions.	You're absolutely right; Tom is impossible to get along with.
Probing	Asks a lot of questions in an attempt to get to the heart of the matter.	When did all this start? What do you want me to do about it?
Smoothing	Pats the speaker on the head and makes light of his or her problems; urges conflict resolution.	You and Tom just had a bad day; don't worry—tomorrow it will all be forgotten.
Empathic/Active	Tries to create an encouraging atmosphere for the speaker to use in expressing and solving the problem; tends to feed back neutral summaries of what they have heard.	It seems that you are troubled by the fact that you and Tom don't get along.

Alternatively, the receiver may perception-check; that is, describe what he or she perceives as the sender's inner state at the time of communication to check his or her understanding of the message. For example, if the sender states, "I don't like the work I am doing," the receiver might check his or her perception of the statement by asking, "Are you dissatisfied with the way you are being treated?" or, "Are you dissatisfied with me as a supervisor?" Note that answers to these two questions will identify different feelings.

A third way of checking communication is through behavior description. Here the individual reports specific, observable actions of others without making accusations or generalizations about their motives, personality, or characteristics. Similarly, description of feelings, where the individual specifies or identifies feelings by name, analogy, or some other verbal representation can increase active listening. For example, to help others understand you as a person, you should describe what others did that affects you personally or as a group member. Then you can let others know as clearly and unambiguously as possible what you are feeling.

COMMUNICATION NETWORKS IN SCHOOLS

Communication is embedded in all school structures. In the traditional classical or bureaucratic model, formal communication channels, or networks, traverse the institution through the hierarchy of authority. Figure 7.3 illustrates a typical school district's formal communication network. Note that the chart delineates the formal communication channels and that every member reports to someone. The directors report to the assistant superintendent for instruction, who, with the assistant superintendent for finance, report to the superintendent. The line of communication from the superintendent to the teachers goes through five hierarchical levels. This is reasonably short and direct for a large school district.

With all organizations, formal restrictions on the communication process are apparent. "Making certain to go through proper channels" and "following the chain of command" are two common expressions that are a reflection of communication in organizations. Three characteristics of school bureaucracies seem particularly critical in communication. They are centralization in the hierarchy, the organization's shape or configuration, and the level of information technology.[15]

The degree that authority is not delegated but concentrated in a single source in the organization is important to the effectiveness of communication systems. In centralized schools, a few positions in the structure have most of the information-obtaining ability. For example, the superintendent and two assistant superintendents pictured in our illustration would gather most of the information for the formal system of communication. If the district is decentralized or loosely coupled, however, the information-obtaining potential is more or less spread across all of the positions. Research examining the different information-obtaining abilities supports the finding that centralized structures are more efficient communicators when the problems and tasks are relatively simple and straightforward. When the problems and tasks become more complex, however, decentralized hierarchies appear to be more efficient. We would argue that since the process of education is by nature complex, communication is an educational setting would be facilitated by a more decentralized structure (social systems or open systems models).

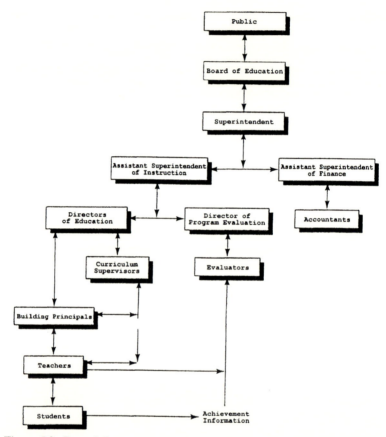

Figure 7.3. *Formal Communication Channels for Program Implementation in a School District.*

The number of hierarchical levels, or tallness versus flatness of the school organization, also affects the communication processes. Hierarchical levels and size are structural characteristics that are commonly associated with the shape of an organization. A school district with five levels, such as the one depicted here, differs from systems with more or fewer levels in its ability to communicate across levels and from top to bottom. The number of levels can be seen as the distance a message must travel. As the distance increases, the chance for message distortion increases, and the satisfaction with the quality and quantity of communication decreases. Teachers will generally express less satisfaction with messages from superintendents than from principals. In addition, organizational size is negatively related to communication quality; as the district becomes larger, communication becomes more impersonal or formal and quality declines. This is part of the reason that the subdividing of large school districts into charter schools and "houses" within schools is proliferating. For communication and other purposes, smaller is better.

Technology also appears to have a significant effect on organizational communication, though that effect remains somewhat speculative. Compared to other organizations, schools, and even colleges, have a relatively low level of technology. However, as communication technology becomes more sophisticated in schools, its use will dramatically alter the communication that takes place in both the formal and informal networks.

We are living in a creative and dynamic era that is producing fundamental changes, as is apparent in such advances as computer networks, electronic mail, computer conferences, communication satellites, data-handling devices and the various forms of distance education. Until recently, electronic information exchange has largely been adapted to convey voice, vision, text, and graphics as distinct and separate types of communication. During the next few years, simultaneous and instantaneous transmission of voice, vision, text, and graphics to many locations will be common. Even imagining these technologies together with the geographic distribution of participants does not adequately capture the differences between these and traditional media. Consequently, the potential influence of such technologies on all aspects of communication in schools is probably underestimated.

EXTERNAL COMMUNICATION

The open-systems model of organizational structure highlights the vulnerability and interdependence of organizations and their environments. External environments are important because they affect the internal structures and processes of organizations; hence, one is forced to look both inside and outside the organization to explain behavior within school organizations. However, the growing necessity to interact with the outside environment places added responsibilities and demands on the school district's communications processes. The need to communicate with parents, government officials, advocacy groups, and the mass media cannot be denied. This necessity, however, is a relatively recent phenomenon and presents difficulties to administrators whose training does not normally include communicating with the public through the mass media.

Although the principles of effective communication still prevail when dealing with the outside community, some nuances need to be stressed. Perhaps the most important aspect of communication that needs to be considered when dealing with the public is the uniformity of the message. The message must be clear and consistent and must emanate from a single source. In these cases, the chain of command and channels of communication need to be well-defined and structured along the lines of the classical model. It is imperative that the school "speak with one voice." Someone in the school district should be designated as the clearinghouse for all external communication. This individual, or office, should review all external communication for clarity and accuracy, and school personnel should be keenly aware of the school's policy with regard to external communication. Thus, although a more loosely structured communication system is very appropriate for internal communication, a more tightly structured one is necessary for effective external communication.

MATRIX DESIGN

To overcome some of the problems inherent in the classical structure of most organizations, including schools, matrix or mixed designs have evolved to improve mechanisms of lateral communication and information flow across the organization.[16]

The matrix organization, originally developed in the aerospace industry, is characterized by a dual authority system. There are usually functional and program or product-line managers, both reporting to a common superior and both exercising authority over workers within the matrix. Typically, a matrix organization is particularly useful in highly specialized technological areas that focus on innovation. But that certainly does not preclude use in those educational settings where creativity and innovation need to be fostered. The matrix design allows program managers to interact directly with the environment vis-à-vis new developments. Usually each program requires a multidisciplinary team approach; the matrix structure facilitates the coordination of the team and allows team members to contribute their special expertise.

The matrix design has some disadvantages that stem from the dual authority lines. Individual workers may find having two supervisors to be untenable since it can create conflicting expectations and ambiguity. The matrix design may also be expensive in that both functional and program managers may spend a considerable amount of time at meetings attempting to keep everyone informed of program activities. A matrix design in a college setting is depicted in Figure 7.4.

The use of matrix design in education is not very common, but it is a viable way of organizing when communication needs to occur outside the "proper channels." The popularity of interdisciplinary and multicultural courses and programs in education has caused an increased interest in matrix design. Many high schools and colleges are informally organized in a matrix design. It would most likely serve these institutions well to consider matrix design as a formal organizational structure, especially in cases when communication problems are evident.

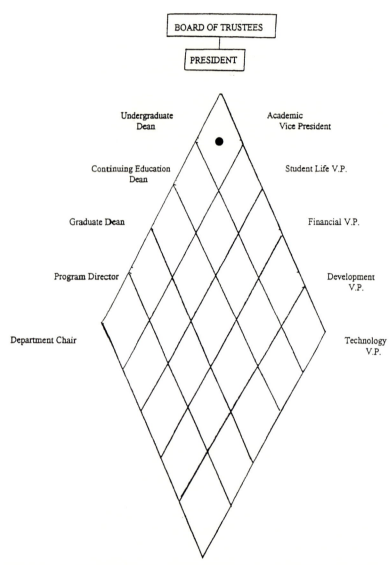

Figure 7.4. *A Matrix Design: A Faculty or Staff Member in This Example Reports to Both the Academic Vice President and the Dean. The Cell That the Individual Is in for a Particular Task Determines the Reporting Relationships.*

A foreign-born plumber in New York once wrote to the Bureau of Standards that he found hydrochloric acid fine for cleaning drains, and he asked if they agreed. Washington replied: "The efficacy of hydrochloric acid is indisputable, but the chlorine residue is incompatible with metallic permanence."

The plumber wrote back that he was mighty glad the Bureau agreed with him.

Considerably alarmed, the Bureau replied a second time: "We cannot assume responsibility for the production of toxic and noxious residues with hydrochloric acid and suggest that you use an alternative procedure."

The plumber was happy to learn that the Bureau still agreed with him.

Whereupon Washington wrote: "Don't use hydrochloric acid; it eats hell out of pipes."

Communicating with ease and clarity is no simple task. There are, however, various theories about how it can be most effectively carried out. Classical theory, social system theory, and open system theory all incorporate a perspective toward the communication process, or, who should say what through which channel to whom and to what effect. Classical theory stresses that the communication process exists to facilitate the manager's command and control over the employees in a formal, hierarchical, and downwardly directed manner. The purpose is to increase efficiency and productivity.

The social system orientation suggests that to be effective, communication has to be two-way and that the meaning of the message is as much to be found in the psychological makeup of the receiver as it is the sender. The channels can be informal as well as formal and include anyone who has an interest in a particular subject.

The open system orientation emphasizes the communication process working toward drawing the various subsystems of an organization into a collaborating whole. Also, drawing the organization's actions into a close fit with the needs of its environment is an essential outcome of the process. This orientation emphasizes that between senders and receivers the communication process must penetrate social class differences, cultural values, time orientations, and ethnocentrism of all types.

None of the conceptual frameworks, by itself, escapes the barriers to communication. The story of the plumber illustrates the problems of message coding, decoding, and transmission. We have suggested that in order for communication to be effective, we should adapt the process to the situation. We have suggested that when communicating with the outside community, a structured process may be appropriate, while when communicating with the inside community, a less structured process may be appropriate. This approach is in concert with one of the underlying themes of this book, that whether we are speaking about organizational structure, leadership, motivation, or communication, we need to adapt the approach or model to the situation in which we find ourselves. Taking a minute each day to obtain feedback regarding the effectiveness of the communication process at an institution is time well spent and will go a long way in ensuring that the process is appropriate in each situation.

DIAGNOSTIC CHECKLIST

Here are some questions that may help in assessing an institution's communication process:

- How effective is the communication process?
- What barriers to communication exist?
- Is the correct communication style utilized under the proper conditions?
- Does communication include feedback, where appropriate?
- Is there a climate of mutual trust and respect?
- Are active listening and other techniques that improve the communication process used?
- Do individuals use assertive, nonassertive, or aggressive communication?

Chapter 8

One-Minute Assessment of the Decision-Making Process

Suppose Will Smith were appointed to the position of superintendent of schools for the Rose Tree School District with the expressed purpose of right-sizing the school district in light of its declining student population. Having been successful in a similar situation in another school district, how should Will Smith proceed?

A good-quality decision brings about the desired result while meeting relevant criteria and constraints. What would constitute a good-quality decision in the situation in Rose Tree School District? Certainly a decision that reduces costs while maintaining educational quality would be considered a good quality one. Also, a decision that meets the needs of those affected by the decision, including students, faculty, staff, administrators, and the taxpayers would qualify. So too would a decision that meets the financial, human, time, and other constraints existing in the situation.

The quality of the decision depends in part on the level of the decision maker's technical or task skills, interpersonal or leadership skills, and decision-making skills. Technical or task skills refer to the individual's knowledge of the particular area in which the decision is being made. In the decision that Will Smith must make about right-sizing, task skills refer to knowledge of labor costs, projected revenues, educational product information, and school system overhead costs. Interpersonal or leadership skills relate to the way individuals lead, communicate with, motivate, and influence others. Will Smith, for example, must be able to get the other stakeholders in the school system to accept the decision for which he is responsible. Effective communication should facilitate understanding and acceptance of the decision in the implementation. Decision-making skills are the basic abilities to perform the components of the decision-making process, including situational analysis, objective setting, and generation, evaluation, and selection of alternatives, as discussed later in this chapter.

Will Smith and any advisors he involves in the decision making must produce a decision that they and the rest of the school system community can accept, one that they are willing to "live with." For example, closing two schools may be a high-quality decision, but the teachers' union may oppose it so much that the union members would cripple the work at other schools. Alternatively, reducing the teaching staff may be a high-quality decision, but the students and parents might resist the change because they feel that they are not receiving a quality education. Thus, *acceptance* of the decision is a characteristic that needs to be considered along with the *quality* of the decision.

VROOM/YETTON DECISION-MAKING MODEL

The administrative and organizational theory literature are in agreement about the two most important factors to be considered in determining the decision style that will produce the most effective decisions. While Vroom and Yetton's model includes the additional dimensions of shared goals and conflict possibility, the two key elements are the quality and the acceptance of the decision, as described above. Figure 8.1 summarizes the identification of the decision style that is most appropriate for particular problem types.

The two key elements are quality, or the likelihood of one decision to be more rational than another, and acceptance, or the extent to which acceptance or commitment on the part of subordinates is crucial to the effective implementation of the decision.

For example, if a new law is passed regarding education and the administrator has to include it in the revised edition of the student handbook, the quality of the decision would be more important than

The administrative and organizational theory literature (Maier 1962; Bridges, 1967; Vroom and Yetton, 1973) are in total agreement about the two most important factors to be considered in determining the decision style which will produce the most effective decisions. While Vroom and Yetton's model adds the additional dimension of shared goals and conflict possibility, the two key elements are also stressed: QUALITY and ACCEPTANCE. The diagram below summarizes Maier's work in identifying the decision style which is most appropriate for particular problem types. The two key elements are defined as:

(1) Quality (Q) - The importance of quality, i.e., one solution is likely to be more rational than another

        The extent to which the leader possesses sufficient information/ expertise to make high-quality decisions by him or herself.

(2) Acceptance (A) - The extent to which acceptance or commitment on the part of subordinates is crucial to the effective implementation of the decision.

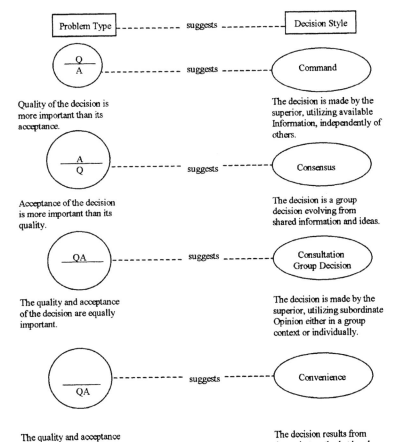

Figure 8.1. *The Dimensions of Effective Decisions.*

its acceptance. Therefore, the appropriate decision style is command. On the other hand, if acceptance is more important than quality, as in the development of a new teacher evaluation instrument, the proper decision style would be consensus.

If both the quality and acceptance are of equal importance, as in whether to adopt a whole language approach to reading, consultation or group decision making would be the appropriate style. Finally, if neither the quality nor the acceptance is important, such as deciding what color to paint the school lockers, convenience would be the applicable style.

ETHICAL DECISION MAKING

In addition to evaluating a decision in terms of its quality and acceptance, we can also assess how well it meets the criteria of ethical fairness and justice. Consider, for example, a disastrous decrease in standardized test scores in a high school. Top administrators are faced with the decision of whether to risk public outrage and the possible transfer of significant numbers of students or ignore the situation.[17]

Administrators and staff can assess whether the decisions they make are ethical by applying personal moral codes or society's code of values. They can apply philosophical views of ethical behavior, or they can assess the potential harmful consequences of behaviors to certain constituencies. One way of thinking about ethical decision making suggests that a person who makes a moral decision must first recognize the moral issue of whether a person's actions can hurt or help others; second, make a moral judgment; third, decide to attach greater priority to more concerns than financial or other concerns, or establish their moral intent; and finally, act on the moral concerns of the situation by engaging in moral behaviors.[18] In making an ethical decision, administrators can use the checklist shown in Figure 8.2.

The decision-making processes described thus far can apply to decisions made by individuals or groups. Yet, group decision making brings different resources to the task than does individual decision making. When a group makes a decision, a synergy occurs that causes the group decision to be better than the sum of the individual decisions. The involvement of more than one individual brings additional

	Yes	No
1. "Does my decision treat me, or my company, as an exception to a convention that I must trust others to follow?"	—	—
2. "Would I repel customers by telling them?"	—	—
3. "Would I repel qualified job applicants by telling them?"	—	—
4. "Have I been cliquish?" (If "Yes," answer questions 4a through 4c. If "No," skip to question 5.)	—	—
4a. "Is my decision partial?"	—	—
4b. "Does it divide the constituencies of the company?"	—	—
4c. "Will I have to pull rank (use coercion) to enact it?"	—	—
5. "Would I prefer to avoid the consequences of this decision?"	—	—
6. "Did I avoid any of the questions by telling myself that I could get away with it?"	—	—

Figure 8.2. General Ethical Checklist. [Reprinted with permission by Jan Press Inc., from M. R. Hyman, R. Skipper, and R. Tansey. Ethical codes are not enough, Business Horizons (March-April 1990), p. 17.]

knowledge and skills to the decision, and it tends to result in higher quality decisions. However, the same caveat holds for decision making, as we have reiterated throughout this book. That is, decision making is situational, and the idiosyncracies of the moment dictate the decision-making approach to be taken. For example, if the school building is on fire, participative decision making is not appropriate.[19]

CULTURAL DIVERSITY

As the group becomes more diverse—attitudinally, behaviorally and culturally—the advantages of cultural diversity increase. Cultural diversity provides the greatest asset for teams with difficult, discretionary tasks requiring innovation. Diversity becomes least helpful when working on simple tasks involving repetitive and routine procedures.[20]

TIME REQUIRED

Group decision making generally takes more time than decision making by individuals. The exchange of information among many individuals, as well as effort spent on obtaining consensus, is time consuming. Sometimes, to reach a decision more quickly or to reach a decision all group members will accept, groups "satisfice" rather than optimize. That is, they tend to make decisions that are expedient.

RISKINESS OF DECISIONS

Early research suggested that groups tend to make riskier decisions. More recent research suggests that this "risky-shift" phenomenon is actually a "polarization" phenomenon. Groups become more extreme in the direction of the initial predominant view. Because no single person shoulders the consequences of the decision made by a group, individuals may feel less accountable and will accept more risky or extreme solutions. When a problem occurs in a school, the parents do not complain to the committee, they complain to the principal. Thus, a committee feels free to make a decision that is more risky.

RECOGNIZING EXPERTISE

Groups may ignore individual expertise, opting instead for group consensus. Particularly as a member of a group of peers, an individual may be reluctant to discriminate among individuals on the basis of their expertise. Groups then may develop "groupthink," a mode of thinking with a norm of concurrence-seeking behavior, as described below. When group members choose a colleague's solution that they consider to be good, the resulting decision equals the quality of a decision obtained by group decision making and is no riskier than a group decision. But the effectiveness of such a "best member strategy" depends on the probability of the group's selecting the real best member and on the potential for subjectivity in the solution. Even then, research suggests that many groups can perform better than the most knowledgeable member.[21]

GROUPTHINK

Irving Janis first identified groupthink as a factor that influenced the misguided 1961 Bay of Pigs invasion. The symptoms of groupthink arise when members of decision-making groups try to avoid being too critical in their judgment of other group members' ideas and focus too heavily on developing concurrence. It occurs most frequently in highly cohesive groups, particularly in stressful situations. For example, group members experiencing groupthink may feel invulnerable to criticism and hence believe that any action they take or decision they make will be positively received. They may also ignore external criticism, choosing instead to rationalize their actions or decisions as optimum. Some group members may also pressure other group members to agree with the group's decision. Deviant opinions are either ignored or not tolerated. Members can neither question views offered nor offer disconfirming information. All of these aspects were present in the Bay of Pigs decision.[22]

CHOOSING GROUP DECISION MAKING

In general, group or individual decision-making choices can be made by considering the type of problem encountered, the importance of its acceptance, the desired solution quality, the individuals involved, the organizational culture, and the time available.

Group decision making is superior when a task or problem requires a variety of expertise, when problems have multiple parts that can be addressed by a division of labor, and when problems require estimates. Individual decision making results in more efficiency if policy dictates the correct solution. Individual decision making also tends to lead to more effective decisions for problems that require completion of a series of complex stages, as long as the individual receives input from many sources, because it allows better coordination of the phases in solving the problem. In Rose Tree School District, for example, the main decision that Will Smith and his colleagues must make is how to reduce costs without reducing quality. This type of problem requires diverse knowledge and skills, creativity, and completion of a series of complex stages, calling most likely for a combination of individual and group decision making.

Group decision making more often leads to acceptance than does decision making by individuals. In addition, since individuals involved in making a decision generally become committed to the decision, use of group consensus expedites acceptance of the decision by the group, thereby increasing individual and group commitment to the decision. Acceptance of the decision about right-sizing at Rose Tree may affect its implementation in the short run, and since school employees cannot easily be replaced, may also affect it in the long run. Therefore, the acceptance is as important as the quality of the decision.

Group decision making generally leads to higher quality solutions unless an individual's expertise in the decision areas is identified in the beginning. At Rose Tree, Will Smith has had successful experience in right-sizing; therefore, he has less need for group input to make a high quality decision. However, he needs the input because the acceptance of the decision is so important.

The personalities and capabilities of the people involved in the decision will help or hinder group decision making. Some individuals have difficulty collaborating in a group setting, whereas others are used to dealing with diverse viewpoints and attitudes. Also, groups

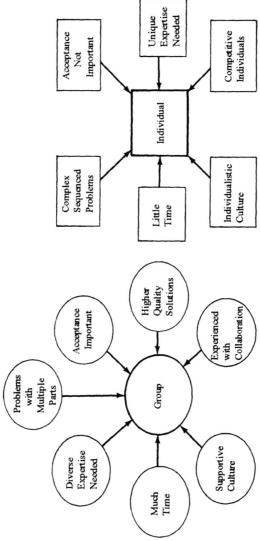

Figure 8.3. Individual versus Group Problem Solving. *(Adapted from Mark Hanson.* Educational Administration and Organizational Behavior. *Boston: Allyn & Bacon, 1991.)*

can ignore individual expertise, creating tension, distrust, and resentment, which can hinder the identification of effective solutions.

The organizational culture provides a context in which the rational or alternative decision-making processes occur. Supportive climates encourage group problem solving; competitive climates stimulate individual responses.

The amount of time available will determine whether group problem solving is feasible because group decision making takes much more time than individual decision making. Rose Tree School District must resolve its problem in a timely manner or risk a taxpayer revolt; therefore, the amount of group participation may be somewhat limited. Figure 8.3 summarizes the advantages and disadvantages of group versus individual decision making.

WAYS TO IMPROVE DECISION MAKING

How can decision makers overcome barriers, reduce biases, and make more effective decisions? There are at least three techniques that can improve decision making: brainstorming, the nominal group technique, and the Delphi technique.

BRAINSTORMING

Groups or individuals use brainstorming when creativity is needed to generate many alternatives for consideration in decision making. In brainstorming, they list as many alternatives as possible without simultaneously evaluating the feasibility of any alternative. For example, Will Smith might charge a task force with listing all the ways of reducing costs in the Rose Tree School District. The absence of evaluation encourages group members to generate rather than defend ideas. Then, after ideas have been generated, they are evaluated and decisions are made. Although brainstorming can result in many shallow and useless ideas, it can also motivate members to offer new ideas. It works best when individuals have a common view of what constitutes a good idea, but it is harder to use when specialized knowledge or complex implementation is required.[23]

NOMINAL GROUP TECHNIQUE

The nominal group technique is a structured group meeting that helps resolve differences in group opinion by having individuals generate and then rank-order a series of ideas in the problem-exploration, alternative-generation, or choice-making stage of group decision making.[24] A group of individuals is presented with a stated problem. Each person individually offers alternative solutions in writing. The group then shares the solutions and lists them on a blackboard or large piece of paper, as in brainstorming. The group discusses and clarifies the ideas. They then rank and vote their preference for the various ideas. If the group has not reached an agreement, they repeat the ranking and voting procedure until the group reaches some agreement.

A more recent version of the nominal group technique emphasizes anonymity of input, pursuing a single purpose at any one group meeting, collecting and distributing inputs before a meeting, and delaying evaluation until all inputs are displayed. It also assures opportunities for discussing displayed items before voting and limiting discussion to their pros and cons, allowing any individual to reword items, always using anonymous voting, and providing a second vote option.

The size of the group and diverse expertise of its members increase the usefulness of the nominal group technique. It encourages each group member to think about and offer ideas about the content of a proposal and then directs group discussion. It moves the group toward problem resolution by focusing on top-ranked ideas and eliminating less valued ones systematically. The nominal group technique also encourages continued exploration of the issues, provides a forum for the expression of minority viewpoints, gives individuals some time to think about the issues before offering solutions, and provides a mechanism for reaching a decision expediently through the ranking-voting procedure. It fosters creativity by allowing extensive individual input into the process. Strong personality types will dominate the group less often because of the opportunity for systematic input by all group members. It encourages innovation, limits conflict, emphasizes equal participation by all members, helps generate con-

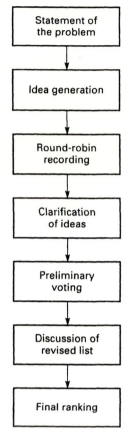

Figure 8.4. *Steps in Nominal Grouping. (Adapted from Judith R. Gordon.* Organizational Behavior, *4th ed. Boston: Allyn & Bacon, 1993.)*

sensus, and incorporates the preferences of individuals in decision-making choices. However, unless the administrator is trained in the use of this technique and the one that follows, it would be more prudent to employ an organizational consultant trained in these techniques to act as a facilitator in the process. Figure 8.4 illustrates the steps in nominal grouping technique.

DELPHI TECHNIQUE

Basically, the Delphi technique structures group communication in dealing with a complex problem in four phases: exploration of the subject by individuals, reaching understanding of the group's view of the issues, sharing and evaluation of any reasons for differences, and final evaluation of all information. In the conventional Delphi, a small group designs a questionnaire, which is completed by a larger respondent group. The results are then tabulated and used in developing a revised questionnaire, which is again completed by the larger group. Thus, the results of the original polling are fed back to the respondent group to use in subsequent responses. This procedure is repeated until the issues are narrowed, responses are focused, or consensus is reached. In another format, a computer summarizes the results and replaces the small group. Such group decision support systems have increased the focus on the task or problem, the depth of analysis, communication about the task, clarifying information and conclusions, effort expended by the group, widespread participation of group members, and consensus reaching.[25]

Delphi is very helpful in a variety of circumstances. First, if the decision makers cannot apply precise analytical techniques to solving the problem but prefer to use subjective judgments on a collective basis, Delphi can provide input from a large number of respondents. Second, if the individuals involved have historically failed to communicate effectively in the past, the Delphi procedures offer a systematic method for ensuring that their opinions are presented. Third, the Delphi does not require face-to-face interaction and thus succeeds when the group is too large for such a direct exchange. Fourth, when time and cost prevent frequent group meetings or when additional pre-meeting communication between group members increases the efficiency of the meeting held, the Delphi technique offers significant value for decision making. Fifth, the Delphi can overcome situations where individuals greatly disagree or where the anonymity of views must be maintained to protect group members. Finally, the Delphi technique reduces the likelihood of groupthink; it prevents one or more members from dominating by their numbers or the strength of their personality. Figure 8.5 summarizes the steps of the Delphi technique.

Decision making is a basic and important process in educational institutions. The success experienced by educational administrators depends largely on their mastery and effective implementation of the

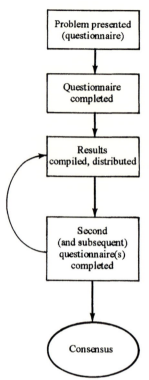

Figure 8.5. Steps in the Delphi Technique. (Adapted from Judith R. Gordon. Organizational Behavior, *4th ed. Boston: Allyn & Bacon, 1993.*)

decision-making process. In this chapter we described the nature of the decision being made in right-sizing the Rose Tree School District. We noted that to make such decisions effective, individuals must have technical, interpersonal, and decision-making skills. We outlined basic decision-making processes that help improve the quality of a decision and encourage its acceptance by others. We noted that quality and acceptance are the two most important factors to be considered in making a decision. Decision makers must systematically analyze the situation; set objectives; generate, evaluate, and select alternatives; make the decision; and evaluate the decision made.

In all of this we stressed the situational nature of effective decision making. There is no single decision-making style that is effective at all times and in all situations.

Next, we compared decision making by individuals and groups.

The advantages and disadvantages of group versus individual decision making were presented, as were the factors that determine the extent of group participation. We concluded by suggesting some techniques to improve decision making, including the nominal group technique, brainstorming, and the Delphi technique. Taking a few minutes each day to determine which decision-making model is best for a given situation is another step leading to effective administration.

DIAGNOSTIC CHECKLIST

Here are some questions that may be helpful in assessing the decision-making process in an institution:

- What type of decisions are being made?
- Do organizational members make high-quality, accepted, and ethical decisions?
- Do decision makers follow the basic process of decision making?
- Is the group appropriately involved in decision making?
- What barriers are there to effective decision making?
- What techniques are being used to overcome these barriers?

Chapter 9

One-Minute Assessment of the Conflict Management Process

A few years ago we invited Dr. Janet Baker, a well-known authority on conflict, to address a group of principals at a Principal's Academy, which we offered at St. Joseph's University in Philadelphia. We introduced Dr. Baker's topic as "conflict resolution." Upon taking the podium, Dr. Baker quickly corrected us and said that she was there to talk about "conflict management, not conflict resolution." "If your goal as a principal is to resolve all conflict, you will be doomed to frustration and failure," she said. "The best that you can hope for is to manage conflict."

Conflict is the result of incongruent or incompatible potential influence relationships between and within individuals, groups, or organizations. Conflict can be public or private, formal or informal, rational or nonrational. The likelihood of conflict increases when parties have the chance to interact, when the parties see their differences as incompatible, and when one or both parties see some utility in engaging in conflict to resolve incompatibility.

Conflict most commonly results from four circumstances. First, when mutually exclusive goals or values actually exist or are perceived to exist by the groups involved, conflict can occur. In the collective bargaining process, for example, the teachers' union may perceive that the administration's goals may conflict with those of the teachers. Second, behavior designed to defeat, reduce, or suppress the opponent may cause conflict. Again, union and management have historically experienced conflict for this reason. Third, groups that face each other with mutually opposing actions and counteractions cause conflict. For example, if the second grade teacher does not follow the curriculum, the third grade teacher will be affected because the students will not have been properly prepared. Finally, if each group attempts to create a relatively favored position, conflict may occur. If the English department attempts to show administration that it is superior to the other departments by demonstrating the others' ineptness, conflict occurs.

Conflict can have functional or dysfunctional outcomes. Whether conflict takes a constructive or destructive course is influenced by the sociocultural context in which the conflict occurs, because differences tend to exaggerate barriers and reduce the likelihood of conflict resolution. The issues involved will also affect the likely outcomes. Whether the parties have cooperative, individualistic, or competitive orientations toward conflict will affect the outcomes as well. Obviously, those with cooperative attitudes are more likely to seek a functional outcome. Characteristics of the conflicting parties also affect conflict behavior. Finally, misjudgments and misperceptions contribute to dysfunctional conflict.

Effective managers learn how to create functional conflict and manage dysfunctional conflict. They develop and practice techniques for diagnosing the causes and nature of conflict and transforming it into a productive force in the organization. Many colleges, for example, have a healthy competition among schools within the university for the recruitment of the most qualified students.

Some conflict is beneficial. It can encourage organizational innovation, creativity, and adaptation. For example, a number of nonpublic school systems, and even some public school systems, allow schools within the system to compete for the same students. This "open enrollment" policy often spawns innovation in marketing techniques, and more importantly, in curriculum and programs. In these cases, conflict can result in more worker enthusiasm and better decisions. Can you think of a situation where such positive outcomes occurred? Perhaps during a disagreement with a colleague you came to hold a different perspective on an issue or learned that your own perceptions or information had been inaccurate.

On the other hand, conflict can be viewed as dysfunctional for organizations. It can reduce productivity, decrease morale, cause overwhelming dissatisfaction, and increase tension and stress in the organization. It can arouse anxiety in individuals, increase the tension in an organizational system and its subsystems, and lower satisfaction. In addition, some people, often the losers in a competitive situation, feel defeated and demeaned. As the distance between people increases, a climate of mistrust and suspicion may arise. Individuals or groups may focus more narrowly on their own interests, preventing the development of teamwork. Production and satisfaction may decline; turnover and absenteeism may increase. Diagnosing the location and type of conflict, as described next, is a first step in managing conflict so that it results in functional outcomes.

Administrators may encourage individuals or groups to use at least five behaviors or strategies for dealing with conflict: avoidance, accommodation, compromise, forcing, and collaborating. These differ in the extent to which they satisfy a party's own concerns and the other party's concerns. For example, a person or group that uses an avoiding mode is unassertive in satisfying its own concerns and uncooperative in satisfying others' concerns. In contrast, a person or group that uses a collaborating mode is assertive and cooperative. These behaviors are illustrated in Figure 9.1.

Each style is appropriate to different situations that individuals or

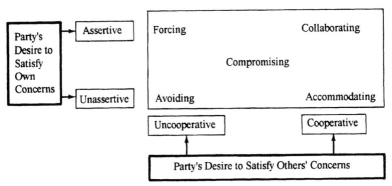

Figure 9.1. *Model of Conflict-Handling Modes. (Adapted from Wayne K. Hay and Cecil G. Miskel.* Educational Administration, *5th ed. New York: McGraw-Hill, 1996.)*

groups face in organizations. Once again, the underlying theme of contingency theory applies.

The behavior an individual or group chooses depends on that party's experiences in dealing with conflict, his or her own personal disposition in interpersonal relations, and the specific elements of a particular conflict episode.

AVOIDANCE

Individuals or groups may withdraw from the conflict situation. They act to satisfy neither their own or the other party's concerns. Avoidance works best when individuals or groups face trivial or tangential issues, when they have little chance of satisfying their personal concerns, when conflict resolution will likely result in significant disruption, or when others can resolve the conflict more effectively. If two secretaries in the secretarial pool, for example, have an argument, the most appropriate strategy for managing the conflict may be avoidance. Let the secretaries resolve the conflict in their own ways. It is like the proverbial story of the next-door neighbors whose children got into an argument, and the adults tried to intervene on behalf of their respective children. The adults ended up being lifelong enemies, and the children were playing with each other again within the hour.

ACCOMMODATION

Individuals or groups who use accommodation demonstrate willingness to cooperate in satisfying others' concerns, while at the same time acting unassertively in meeting their own. Accommodating individuals often smooth over conflict. This mode builds social credits for later issues, results in harmony and stability, and satisfies others. An assistant principal may capitulate on a disagreement with the principal over a minor matter in hopes that he or she can prevail on a larger issue in the future, thus building political capital to be used later.

COMPROMISE

The compromise mode represents an intermediate behavior between the assertiveness and cooperation dimensions. It can include sharing of positions but not moving to the extremes of assertiveness or cooperation. Hence, it often does not maximize satisfaction of both parties. In one study, compromisers had a different communication style from avoiders; they were more likely to focus on communicating information about the job product or plan than messages about rules, regulations, or policies. This style works well when goals are important but not sufficiently important for the individual or group to be more assertive, when the two parties have equal power, or when significant time pressure exists. For example, if two grade partners disagree over which supplementary materials should be used for a certain lesson, they may compromise and use some of each teacher's suggestions.

FORCING

Using the forcing mode, a party tries to satisfy its own concerns while showing an unwillingness to satisfy the other's concerns to even a minimal degree. This strategy works well in emergencies, on issues calling for unpopular actions, and in cases when one party is correct in its position or has much greater power. For example, if a child tries to commit suicide, the principal may wish to inform the parents immediately, and the guidance counselor may wish it to remain confidential. If the principal arbitrarily informs the parents, he or she is using a forcing behavior.

COLLABORATING

The collaboration mode emphasizes problem solving with a goal of maximizing satisfaction for both parties. It means seeing conflict as natural, showing trust and honesty toward others, and encouraging the airing of every person's attitudes and feelings. Each party exerts both assertive and cooperative behavior. Parties can use it when their objectives are to learn, to use information from diverse sources, and to find an integrative solution. If the teachers' union and the school board establish a mutually satisfactory way of working together, they are taking a collaborative or problem-solving approach to resolve or avoid conflict.

Table 9.1. Uses of the Five Conflict Modes.

Conflict-Handling Modes	Appropriate Situations
Competing	1. When quick, decisive action is vital—e.g., emergencies.
	2. On important issues where unpopular actions need implementing—e.g., cost cutting, enforcing unpopular rules, discipline.
	3. On issues vital to company welfare when you know you're right.
	4. Against people who take advantage of noncompetitive behavior.
Collaborating	1. To find an integrative solution when both sets of concerns are too important to be compromised.
	2. When your objective is to learn.
	3. To merge insights from people with different perspectives.
	4. To gain commitment by incorporating concerns into a consensus.
	5. To work through feelings which have interfered with a relationship.
Compromising	1. When goals are important, but not worth the effort or potential disruption of more assertive modes.
	2. When opponents with equal power are committed to mutually exclusive goals.
	3. To achieve temporary settlements to complex issues.
	4. To arrive at expedient solutions under time pressure.
	5. As a backup when collaboration or competition is unsuccessful.
Avoiding	1. When an issue is trivial, or more important issues are pressing.
	2. When you perceive no chance of satisfying your concerns.
	3. When potential disruption outweighs the benefits of resolution.
	4. To let people cool down and regain perspective.
	5. When gathering information supersedes immediate decision.
	6. When others can resolve the conflict more effectively.
	7. When issues seem tangential or symptomatic of other issues.
Accommodating	1. When you find you are wrong—to allow a better position to be heard, to learn, and to show your reasonableness.
	2. When issues are more important to others than yourself—to satisfy others and maintain cooperation.
	3. To build social credits for later issues.
	4. To minimize loss when you are outmatched and losing.
	5. When harmony and stability are especially important.
	6. To allow subordinates to develop by learning from mistakes.

Source: Adapted from Wayne K. Hoy and Cecil G. Miskel. *Educational Administration,* 5th ed. New York: McGraw-Hill, 1996.

Conflict frequently characterizes individuals and groups in organizations. It can exist at the intrapersonal, interpersonal, intragroup, intergroup, intraorganizational, and interorganizational levels. As a dynamic force, conflict progresses from latent to perceived, felt, and manifest stages, and finally to a conflict aftermath. Its consequences can be functional, such as increased creativity and exchange of ideas, or dysfunctional, such as increased stress, absenteeism, and turnover or decreased satisfaction and performance.

Interacting groups are especially prone to conflict. Effective intergroup relations require managers and other organizational members to diagnose the extent and causes of their interdependence. Groups can demonstrate pooled, sequential, reciprocal, or team interdependence. Groups experiencing reciprocal or team interdependence more often experience dysfunctional conflict and other problems than those showing pooled or sequential interdependence. The uses of the five conflict modes are summarized in Table 9.1.

Conflict can be caused by scarce resources, jurisdictional ambiguities, communication breakdowns, personality clashes, power and status differences, and goal differences. However, we have a variety of strategies at our disposal for managing conflict. Conflict can be managed by applying the appropriate intervention style to the situation. Conflict intervention styles such as avoidance, compromise, forcing, accommodation, and collaboration can be applied depending on the vagaries of the situation. The ten-minute administrator will serve him- or herself well to take time each day to determine if the appropriate intervention strategy is being utilized to manage the institution's conflicts.

DIAGNOSTIC CHECKLIST

Here are some questions that may help you assess the conflict management capabilities of your institution:

- Is the conflict in the institution functional or dysfunctional?
- Are there mechanisms for effectively managing conflict and stress?
- Do the mechanisms reflect the situational nature of conflict resolution?
- Are avoidance, compromise, competition, accommodation, and collaboration utilized in the appropriate situations?

What I have attempted to do in this book is to provide a corollary to Blanchard and Johnson's *One Minute Manager* by suggesting that taking ten minutes each day to assess ten important components of effective leadership is a worthwhile exercise. Together, they complete the jigsaw puzzle of effective school management. My opinion is that these ten principles are equally applicable to educational and non-educational administration. However, my only extensive first-hand experience is the field of educational management, where I have seen this approach work effectively time after time. It is my sincere hope that it works for you.

1. Max de Pree, *Leadership is an Art* (New York: Dell Publishing, 1989).

2. K.H. Blanchard and S. Johnson, *The One Minute Manager* (New York: Morrow Publishing, 1982).

3. *Ibid*, p. 17.

4. *Ibid*, p. 32.

5. E.L. Thorndike, *Behaviorism* (New York: Norton, 1924): B.F. Skinner, *The Behavior of Organisms: An Experimental Approach* (New York: Appleton-Century, 1938).

6. Max de Pree, *Leadership Is an Art* (New York: Dell Publishing, 1989).

7. S.A. Kirkpatrick and E.A. Locke, Leadership: Do traits matter? *Academy of Management Executive*, 5 (2) (1991): 49.

8. P. Hersey and K.H. Blanchard, *Management of Organizational Behavior*, 5th Edition (Englewood Cliffs, N.J.: Prentice Hall, 1988).

9. R.J. House, Theory of charismatic leadership. In J.G. Hunt and Larson, eds., *Leadership: The Cutting Edge* (Carbondale, Ill.: Southern Illinois U. Press, 1977).

10. Lee B. Bolman and Terrance E. Deal, *Reframing Organizations* (San Francisco: Jossey Bass, 1991).

11. Kurt Lewin, *Field Theory in Social Science* (New York: Harper and Row, 1951).

12. R.E. Zuker, *Mastering Assertiveness Skills* (New York: AMACOM, 1938), p. 79.

13. *Ibid*, p. 84.

14. A.J. Lange and P. Zakubowski, *Responsible Assertive Behavior* (Champaign, Ill.: Research Press, 1976).

15. Wayne K. Hoy and Cecil G Miskel, *Educational Administration: Theory, Research and Practice*, 5th Edition (New York: McGraw-Hill, Inc., 1996).

16. Charles H. Kepner and Benjamin B. Tregoe, *The Rational Manager* (Princeton, N.J.: Princeton Research Press, 1981).

17. L.K.Trevino, Ethical decision making in organizations: A person-situation interactionist model, *Academy of Management Review,* 11 (1986): 601–617.

18. J.R. Rest, *Moral Development: Advances in Research and Theory* (New York: Praeger, 1986); T.M. Jones, Ethical decision making by individuals in organizations: An issue-contingent model, *Academy of Management Review,* 16 (2) (1991): 366–395.

19. P.C. Nutt, Types of organizational decision processes, *Administrative Science Quarterly,* 29 (1984): 414–450.

20. G. Whyte, Groupthink reconsidered, *Academy of Management Review,* 14 (1989): 40–56; Lamm and Myers, Group induced polarization.

21. K. Dion, R. Baron, and N. Miller, Why do groups make riskier decisions than individuals? In L. Berkowitz, ea., *Advances in Experimental Social Psychology,* vol. 5 (New York: Academic Press, 1970), presents some of the earliest work in this area: see Bazerman, *Judgment in Managerial Decision Making,* for recent discussion of this phenomenon.

22. Judith R. Gordon, *A Diagnostic Approach to Organizational Behavior,* 4th Edition (Boston: Allyn and Bacon, 1993).

23. J.L. Adams, *The Care and Feeding of Ideas: A Guide to Encouraging Creativity* (Reading, Mass.: Addison-Wesley, 1986).

24. L.K. Michaelson, W.E. Watson, and R.H. Black, A realistic test of individual versus group consensus decision making, *Journal of Applied Psychology,* 74 (5) (1989): 834–839.

25. G.P. Huber, *Managerial Decision Making* (Glenview, Ill.: Scott Foresman, 1980); and A. Delbecq, A. Van de Ven, and D. Gustafson, *Group Techniques for Program Planning* (Glenview, Ill.: Scott, Foresman, 1975).